My Rocky Ride Through Life

By
Reg Hughes

MAPLE
PUBLISHERS

My Rocky Ride Through Life

Author: Reg Hughes

Copyright © 2024 Reg Hughes

The right of Reg Hughes to be identified as author of this work has been asserted by the author in accordance with section 77 and 78 of the Copyright, Designs and Patents Act 1988.

First Published in 2024

ISBN 978-1-83538-261-5 (Paperback)
978-1-83538-262-2 (E-Book)

Book Cover Design and Book Layout by:
White Magic Studios
www.whitemagicstudios.co.uk

Published by:
Maple Publishers
Fairbourne Drive, Atterbury,
Milton Keynes,
MK10 9RG, UK
www.maplepublishers.com

A CIP catalogue record for this title is available from the British Library.

All rights reserved. No part of this book may be reproduced or translated in any form or by any means, electronic or mechanical, including photocopying, recording or by any information storage and retrieval system without written permission from the author.

The views expressed in this work are solely those of the author and do not necessarily reflect the publisher's opinions, and the publisher, as a result of this, disclaims any responsibility for them.

CONTENTS

Chapter 1 – Start in life, business startup and breakin........4

Chapter 2 – Building up the business 17

Chapter 3 – The cancer................................31

Chapter 4 – Dive boat trip to the red sea 45

Chapter 5 – Daughter karen's wedding...............54

Chapter 6 – Shooting and fishing........................65

Chapter 7 – Prank on Vince.............................75

Chapter 8 – Brake pads..................................78

Chapter 9 – Spoof...81

Chapter 10 – Holidays 83

Chapter 11 – Lufapak......................................91

Chapter 12 – Lin's health 94

Chapter 13 – Cottage flooding 96

Chapter 14 – Workshop fire..............................97

Chapter 1

START IN LIFE, BUSINESS STARTUP AND BREAKIN

My mother's maiden name was Barbara Patricia Cochrane Le Mare.

The family originated in France and came over to England in the 1800's, and started a family business in London, and the north of England in the silk weaving industry.

Some members of the family then left England and went to various parts of the world.

In 1918 four members of the family went and started a ranch in the northern Mexico state of Coahuila, but were murdered and thrown down a well on their ranch by Mexican bandits.

My mother lived with her parents and they had a chauffeur and gardener called William Hughes, and eventually they married, and moved to a small village in Hockley Heath in Warwickshire.

I was born on the 19th April 1941, one of five in the family, me being the middle member.

I had two brothers and two sisters, but one sister had meningitis when she was two and a half which left her stone deaf, and the other sister was born mentally retarded, but both brothers, like myself, were fine and in good health.

My father worked for the Land Rover operation in Solihull in the early 50's and he was the parts manager, supervising all the spare parts that were shipped to the dealers and abroad.

My mother was an incredible lady looking after all the family, and coping with all the problems, including the second world war, with all its problems and food shortages, but we always had food on the table.

I remember in the latter part of the second world war as a very young boy, I woke up to hear some very load bang so close to the house. I looked out of the window and saw an anti-aircraft gun on the road outside the house firing up into the sky.

We all went different ways, with my brothers going to primary schools and then moving on, and my deaf sister going to a deaf school in Birmingham, and my younger sister being looked after by my mother.

At the age of 14 I had to have an operation to have a testicle put down and after the operation in the QE in Birmingham, they discharged me but called me back, when it was discovered that they had left a swab inside my body, so I had to have an emergency operation to remove it which left my stomach well scarred, and a very serious health condition.

After I recovered, I was then sent to a rehabilitation home on South Devon, to a place called Hilloway, in a village called Stoke-In-Teignhead, where I was looked after for 13 weeks before returning to home, recovered, but weak.

After I left grammar school, I was not happy at home, and eventually left home after falling out with my father, so along with a friend, Will Carter, we left and moved to Shaldon in South Devon, where we had a job to find lodgings and a job.

Eventually I found one bedroom lodgings, and Will found a small chalet in the back garden of a family in the village.

We both ran out of money and had to do all sorts of odd jobs to get some cash, and we finished up by living on cabbages, which we pinched from the fields, for a period of 13 weeks, before we both managed to get jobs.

We boiled, grilled and fried them, and I have have NEVER eaten cabbages since!

I managed to get a job with a Wine and Spirits merchant in Teignmouth as a drivers mate, delivering beers and spirits to all the pubs in the region.

Will managed to get a job as a deck chair attendant on the beaches in Torquay.

This carried us on for a period, and then Will told me that he was going back home, as could could not cope any more.

I stayed on and eventually met Lin who had moved down from London with her family after they purchased a small hotel in Shaldon called the Glenside Hotel.

We went out together from then on, and I changed jobs and started work in and engineering factory called Centrax, in Newton Abbot, which produced turbo blades for the aeronautic industry. My wage was then £13.25 a week.

We then decided to get married on the 13th October 1962, in the church on the bridge in Shaldon, and the service was carried out by an ex vicar, called Percy, who was staying at the Glenside with his wife, so I asked him to carry out the service, which was agreed after he obtained permission from the church

At the reception back at the hotel, Lin's father stood up and said in his speech...I have had her for 18 years and now it's your turn.....and sat down!!

Later that evening, the vicar's wife told me that Percy was going to bed as he was tired, and took him off singing, as he was very merry!!

The party went on till quite late, and then the next morning, Lin and I left for our honeymoon, in a hire car, and loads of goods trailing from the back, which I soon discarded about 5 miles down the road.

We spent our honeymoon in Newquay, and had a lovely time, and the weather was kind to us as well.

Our son Paul was born on the 21st November 1963, (the day after President Kennedy was shot) in Newton Abbot hospital, and we were so glad to get him back home to the hotel.

I was getting very bored with all the 3 shift work at Centrax, so we made a decision to move back up to the midlands, as we could earn more money there, and we had an invitation from my deaf sister and deaf husband to live with them in their bungalow in Henley-In Arden.

My father and I started to get back to a normal relationship then and I managed to get a job with a friend of his, Geoff Saunders, who had a small business, and so started to work for him in a small unit packaging spare parts for Lucas Lighting.

We then managed to buy a semi-detached house in Henley-In Arden, with a mortgage, and although it was tight for money, we just about managed.

Then very soon Karen was born on the 7th May 1965, and it all became very tight for money.

The company then expanded and moved to Redditch, where I was made operations director, and the business started to flourish.

Lin also worked for the company running the wages office in Studley

Geoff then promised me a 20% shareholding in the business if it carried on in the same way, so that was a very good incentive.

However he then brought his son Robert into the business as he had just left the Merchant Navy and wanted a job. This worked well for a long period, and the company expanded with other contracts, and one evening Robert told me that I was to get down to Banbury and open up a factory there that he had just negotiated for a new contract with Unipart, who worked for the Rover group.

The contract was to pack all the small fixings for the new Morris Marina, so we had to have a holding warehouse with 645 bin fronts containing all the parts, and pick and pack them and ship them to Seneffe in Belgium where they manufactured the vehicle

I had to hold interviews in a hotel in Banbury, as we needed 35 female packers and 8 male operators, as we were due to open the factory unit within 3 working weeks.

This went very well after a rocky start and as the build quantity increased so did the amount of parts requiring to be packed and shipped.

As the factory had not been used for about 3 years, everyone in Banbury used to park their cars on the front car park, and go off shopping or whatever.

One day a guy parked his car and he had been told several times that we were now operating from there, and it was private property, so please do not park again.

One of the workforce came to my office, and said he is here again, and has left his car on the front, so I told him to block the car in with a stack of metal pallets, and when he came back, to send him into my office.

I kept him waiting and then told him that if it happened again I would get the police to impound the vehicle, as the police station was directly opposite.

He then left and went on his way.

We were always having visits from Unipart inspectors, checking the quality of the parts and also the quality of our packing.

One day we had a visit from the purchase manager and his number 2 and after the meeting, I suggested that the Unipart guys with myself could go to lunch at a little pub I had found quite close.

We got there and as I was asking the guys what they would like to drink, I turned round to order and the guy behind the bar asked me...."And yours sir?!!!"...it turned out that the problem guy parking his car was the landlord. It resulted that after that meet, we became very good friends.

Another day I had one of the foremen in the factory come to see me and told me that the cleaner lady was taking the coffee from the vending machine and putting it into her handbag.

I had a camera fitted and the next time she did it, we had her on camera, so I called her into the office and said she had 2 choices....1... to hand in her notice and that would be it, or... 2... I would take her over the police station and give them all the details. She chose to quit and that I thought was that.

At about 5.30 that evening my office door crashed down and a huge guy stood in the doorway, asking if my name was Hughes, to which I replied yes.

He then came at me and chased me round and round the desk, resulting in me running out of the office and surrounding myself with 3 guys from the factory.

One phoned the police and it took 3 coppers to take him over to the station, and a very close call.

I later found out that he was the heavyweight boxing champion for the Banbury and Oxford area, so a very close call!!

I then had chance to interview a manager who started the next month, so I then moved back to the Redditch operation, which was now getting very busy with new contracts from various companies for contract packing.

The packing contracts increased, and the types of parts also, we had to pack and ship to the various warehouses, we required a lot of hired transport, so Robert decided to set up his own transport company.

This worked very well and saved the company a lot of money.

The Unipart operation then became the main part of the business as they decided to give us the contract for all the packaging of their parts.

Robert was getting to be more of a problem for me, and he loved to call me at all hours of the day or night, to either drive him to a meeting or pick him up from a restaurant after a meal with customers.

One night I was in bed and received a phone call from him saying that he was at home and had people trying to break in the house, so I got dressed and drove quickly to his house.

I ran in and he was sitting in a chair looking quite drunk with a large glass of whisky, and said come and have a drink. I ran over and hit him and knocked him off the chair and said... "Don't you ever do that to me again".

One day he came into the factory and called me into his office and stated that although his father and promised me shares, I would never receive them, as the company was called G.L.Saunders and it would not have a Hughes member in it.

After that I was resigned to look for something else to start my own company, and as all I really knew was about packaging, I thought I would leave and start my own operation.

I spoke to my Unipart contacts, who had by then become very good friends as well as business contacts. We used to have weekends with the purchase director his wife and children, his manager and his wife, together with Lin and our children.

We went for weekends to Paris several times and also to Legoland in Denmark, as well as weekends in hotels in the UK, and had some really good times.

I told them that I was not enjoying life at the company, and thought that I would start my own company. They said that they would help with whatever they could, if I did decide to do it, and started by putting my company name on their computer.

I then went and had a meeting with Robert, and told him that I was giving him notice to leave the company, and he asked me what I was going to do.

I said that the only thing I knew was packaging so I would start in a small way, with a different type of packing.

So I started the company named Avonvale Packaging Ltd.

I had by then been talking with contacts from Halfords, Terry's springs and also Hydrovane, so were able to gain some business from these companies.

I left the company and rented a small 6000 square feet building in Alcester, and was able to get some staff fairly quickly.

Lin was company director and looked after the accounts, with another member of staff.

I managed to get a loan from the bank to enable me to purchase some skin packing and blister packing machinery, and so we commenced the operation and actually started to make a profit in the second month of operation.

We gradually got small increases from all three companies, so we carried on as that for some time.

I then managed to obtain a new contract with a company who imported woodscrews from China in bulk, and we had to pack them in small cartons of 200 for resale.

This required a different type of machine, which was a weigh-count machine, so the screws were tipped into a bulk hopper, and then it weighed and counted 200 which then it released into the carton held under the machine by an operator.

I knew a guy very well who made these machines in Redditch and so I spoke with him and he said he would supply me with a machine and I could pay him in instalments as I could, which was a great help with cashflow.

This became a nice steady contract and continued for about 18 months, until one day the managing director drove down and came into my office and said I am very sorry, but I have just put the company into receivership.

It was a big shock and he said he would be in touch with me within the week, as he still owed us at that point about £13850.

He left and I phoned my solicitor who told me to put immediately put a lien on the goods we had in stock, which meant that no-one could remove them.

I was wondering whether I would get the money owing and it was very worrying.

I then received a phone call from an Irishman, who told me that he had been informed about the company going into receivership, and he said that his company worked for them and was also owed money, amounting to just over £10000.

He asked me what stock we had of his goods, as he would collect them and ship them to Ireland and if possible we could both clear our debts.

I worked out that we had about £24500 in value in our warehouse and we agreed that he would send containers over to collect the goods if we agreed.

I got my solicitor to draw up an agreement and things started moving quickly, and the next morning we had 2 containers arrive and we loaded all the product into the containers.

He then came with me to the bank and transferred the £13850 which was owed to us, and we shook hands and he left and flew back to Ireland.

In that week, the receiver phoned me and asked me what stocks we had of the companies product. I said we had none on site as we had packed all the stock we had prior to the company going into receivership. They said they would come the next morning to inspect the warehouse, and I told them they would be very welcome. They arrived and confirmed that we did not have any product and left us in peace. A very lucky escape!!

I was always in touch with my Unipart friends, and had a call from them to say that to get any business from them I had to get my company name onto their computer system. I said so what do I do to get that, and was told that they would give me a very nasty small job to get things started.

This turned out to be what they called a "Parts Bar Unit", which consisted of a wooden display unit, which had to be erected, together with packing all the spare parts for the unit, which then would be shipped to the dealers for display within their sales showrooms.

He told me the price I could charge, which just about covered the operation, and so we did this, and then had our name on their system, for any future business.

Little did I know what was about to happen in the near future!!!

The following month, I had a phone call to inform me from the police that our factory unit had been broken into.

I arrived at the site to find that some guys had entered the unit through the roof, and smashed every machine we had, including our typewriters in the office.

Our lady supervisor was there also, as they had heard, and a few of our lady packers.

I was in tears and thought we might as well lock the doors as we were finished!

However the police arrived and news reporters and also men from other units on the estate, who offered to help with anything we wanted them to do, but it was such a mess to clear, with everyone joining in.

It turned out that we appeared on Police 5, which was a TV programme held by Shaw Taylor, to help with local crime, and they showed all the damage in the factory, asking anyone for information on the crime.

The next day I had a call from the police who wanted to have a chat with me.

I met with DI Roy Brown and we chatted about the break in, and he told me that I must know who did this, and I said that I did have a suspicion that it may be connected with Robert, and he said he would follow it up.

The next evening I went to the Green Dragon pub to have a drink with my pal Joe Turner, and we chatted about the problem I had, and he told me that it must be Robert. He did have a very friendly police sergeant from Redditch police and he used to do anything for Robert if he needed any assistance in any direction.

He even used to go on holiday with Robert, which I know was paid for by the company.

Anyway we then ordered another drink and as I stood up to pay for them, a guy came past me and brushed against me and said" Get out of packaging otherwise you are dead", and then disappeared out of the door.

I told Joe what had happened and he said that just proves what I said about Robert.

The next day I had a phone call and the same message was told to me, but with an addition that if I didn't, my wife and kids would be in danger as well.

I told DI Roy Brown about this and he said be very careful where and what you do in the near future. He said I know you go to the Green Dragon every night for a drink, so when you come out of the pub, just make sure nobody is about, and check all round and under your car!!

Then for the next 6 weeks, I had a phone call every day warning me again, and now and again a guy would bump into me and tell me again to get out of packaging.

I was so worried and did not tell Lin as she would have never coped with it, so in the end I was getting so wound up, that I phoned a friend of mine called Joe wills who had contacts with Boss guns, and asked him if he could get me a revolver, which he did and I kept it under my seat in the car

The phone calls kept coming and I was getting more worried by the day and thought if anyone tries to attack me I would shoot at their legs or someway to harm them.

One evening I left the Green dragon and started on my way home, and turning into the lane towards my house a car was stopped in the road, and a man was on the floor in front of it.

I stopped and ran over to the man and before I knew what was happening I was knocked to the floor and after such a commotion, I got up and the car and man were both gone.

I checked under my seat and the revolver had gone, so I wondered what the hell had happened but went home and didn't mention anything to Lin.

The next day I had a phone call from DI Roy Brown saying that he wanted to see me urgently. I went to his office and when I opened the door I saw my revolver on his table. He told me to sit down and then told me that he was running the show and get rid of that revolver or I will get rid of you for a few years. I apologised and left with the revolver and gave it back to my friend Joe.

We managed to get the factory going again, with the help of many people who were a godsend with all types of help.

A competitor of mine in packaging phoned me from Oxford, and said he had heard of my break in, and that my machinery was all smashed, and he could help as he had a spare Soag skin pack machine if I wanted, but it did need a bit of repair.

I asked him how much he wanted and he said nothing at all just take it away. I thanked him profusely and drove down in a lorry to collect it, and got it back to the factory, and with a friend of mine we worked all night and managed to get it working, so it went back into production the next day.

After about 5 weeks, DI Roy Brown told me that they had arrested the 2 guys who did the actual break in, but didn't get any further with the real people behind the job. He said they had been paid £500 each to do the job, and they were given a prison sentence of 4 years. He said that they were still working on the job and would keep me in touch.

Chapter 2

BUILDING UP THE BUSINESS

We managed to get the business back on track and the phone calls stopped, and I was so relieved.

About another 3 months passed and I had a phone call from my friend at Unipart to say that they would like a meeting with me then next evening at the Lygon Arms at Broadway. I told him that we were due to go away for a few days and he said "Cancel it and be there"

I arrived at the due time and waited for him to arrive, only to find that there were more people than just him.

There was the Managing director, the Purchase director, the Commercial director and the Operations director, and I was wondering what this was all about.

They then told me that they were very worried about the Robert Saunders operation, and having checked their financial situation, they thought that they could be in danger of the company going into receivership.

I asked then how does that affect me, and they said that I knew their business, and would I like to be prepared to set up and take on the work.

I told them that to do that it would need a big factory unit, together with a large staff, and I did not have either, and especially I could not fund it.

They said what do you need…we will help you to set it up, should it happen. I was speechless and said I would need to think about it to determine what I would need. They gave me a week to go back to them with my answer.

At the next meeting, I said that I had found a factory unit of 40,000 square feet in Redditch, and if the Saunders operation went bust, I would be able to get the staff I needed from them. I also told them that I could not get the financial backing needed, and they told me that they would be prepared to give me the monies required up front.

They told me to be ready, as it could happen at any time soon.

I then had a phone call 4 weeks later, to inform me that the company had gone into administration, and so all speed was needed to get things moving. They then transferred all the finance I needed to commence the work to get the factory open and all the machinery.

I then advertised for staff and most of the existing employees applied, so I was able to pick the people I required.

Things then started to happen at such a speed, and we held meetings with Unipart and the administrators, to enable us to transfer all stock and packaging material to our new factory unit.

Within 3 weeks we were up and running, albeit with only part of the total business, but at least Unipart were able to supply their dealers with parts.

Over the next 3 months, the remainder of the business was transferred, and we were working 24/7 to settle everything in and get the business on track again.

One of the biggest problems was to install a new computer system, so I found a self employed software engineer, who started to put together the system that I wanted to handle this new part of the business. I told him what I wanted and he wrote the software and very soon we had the system up and running, which made things a lot easier.

Unipart paid me up front every month, and if I needed anything more, I only had to talk with them and they provided the necessary.

Lin was also very busy running the wages and accounts department, and mainly with manual entries, until we could install a computer system to handle all this part of the business.

We then started on the project of rebuilding our cottage, and although it took about 7 months, we had a completely new cottage, extended in length and extended out front too, with a new garage and annexe.

As the factory unit was not far from the cottage, I used to go home every lunchtime to see how things were going with the building work, and one day I drove into the drive and as I got out of the car, I saw a workman tumbling off the roof, which was not very high, on to the lawn.

I then spoke with the foreman and asked what had happened, and he told me that a local man had visited a few times, chatting with the men, and told them that he made his own cider, which they all asked him to bring.

He had brought some for them to drink, and it was very strong stuff and so the guy that fell off the roof was drunk, along with 3 other guys. The foreman had then phoned his company to arrange for a minibus to come and collect them to take them home.

I knew exactly who this cider maker was, and the next evening I went into the local pub and saw Norman Freeman sitting by the bar and went over to him and kindly asked him not to take any more cider down to the workmen, as they were all drunk when I got there. He smiled and told me they thought they were drinkers, so I had to prove them wrong!!

I first used the local pub, when we moved to the cottage in 1975. All the locals used the pub, and they had a darts team and pool team, and there were most weekends four old guys playing cribbage in the corner

One of the old regulars asked me if I wanted and meat for the weekend, as he had contacts at a butcher in Bromsgrove.

I told him that a nice English leg of lamb would be good, so he said leave it to me.

I went to the pub on the Saturday and he said he had my meat, so I went outside to his van and he had it wrapped up for me, and I paid him

On Sunday when we were preparing for lunch, I unwrapped the meat, only to find that it had New Zealand stamped all over it.

I went into the pub the next evening and told him about it and his reply was "You must have had the wrong one" !!

The operation at the factory went well and after a further 8 months, I was able to step back and able to employ a manager to be in charge of the factory.

I then had a call from my Unipart friend, who told me that Rover were interested in looking for a contract packer to deal with a new operation which was CKD of vehicles (Complete Knock Down).

I had an appointment with the purchase director of Rover who gave me the outline details which was to receive, store, pick and pack parts for the Rover SD1 which were to be shipped to India for assembly there, putting their own engine into the unit.

We received a complete set of parts to establish what was required in the way of storage and handling and also to get the wooden packing cases to ship the parts in.

This was quite a complicated quotation, but we managed to put in a quote, which after some negotiation was accepted. This also meant that we had to have another factory unit, so I hunted about to get one, and finished up with a 30,000 square feet warehouse on Stratford –Upon-Avon, which was previously used by the army for their stores, so we had some fortune in being able to get quite a lot of storage bins which were not used, which they left in the warehouse.

We had a commencement date, so we were able to get staff, and a new manager who had past experience of CKD. We also had to get all the equipment ready in time for this date, and along with a Rover Inspector on site, we commenced this new venture.

We had to prepare and pack a trial pack which was accepted by the on site inspector, and then we were ready to go with a month schedule.

We had been packing and shipping for a period of about 9 months, when I had a call from the Quality manager to inform me that the Standard Motor Company of India was claiming shortages on our packs, so we had a meeting with them to discuss this problem, and they gave us the details of the parts that they were claiming shortages on, which turned out to be the complete front fascia panel.

We could only get 12 of these units into the wooden packing case, so after checking all our pack sheets, we were very confident that we did not have a problem.

Rover then told me that we would need to visit the factory in India and resolve the problem, so they arranged the trip and told me that if it was found to be our problem, then we would have to pick up the tab for the trip and the cost of the parts involved.

My manager and myself flew along with the Rover Quality guys to Dehli, where we have a day before onward flight to Madras. We went to the hotel and after checking in to the room, and it was essential to go to the bar for a reviver!.

It was a superb rooftop bar and the guy behind the bar was dressed like an Indian rajah.

He asked us what we would like to drink and I asked for a beer, so he got a beer and put the bottle down on the bar counter, about to take the top off, when the phone rang so he want to answer the phone. He was some time on the phone, so I took the bottle myself and took the top off and poured it into the glass and drank half the contents He came back and said"Oh dear Saab...what have you done?". I told him that we were thirsty and needed a drink, and he then told me I should have poured the preservative from the top of the bottle first!!.

You can imagine what I was doing for most of the night!!

The next morning, as we were not due to fly until late afternoon, the Rover guys had organised to trip to tour the city with a guide they had sorted. They called him the culture vulture, and he showed us round parts of the city which was very interesting. He then took as to a temple, and said we were going round the back of it, and we were not to use any cameras.

As we commenced to get to the rear of the building I could smell a strange smell, and as we got to the back I could see a fire with smoke and some people lined up by it.

When we got closer we could see a large fire and one guy standing by the fire and one of the people kneeling by the fire and holding his arm out over the fire an on some blocks. The guy then raised his arm and chopped the hand off from the wrist with an axe, and threw the hand on the fire, and then cauterising the joint ,which was the stench we could smell.

Some people were having the feet chopped off, instead of hands

I told the guide that I could not watch this, as it was unhuman, and turned and with our other guys we went back to the front of the cathedral, and asked the guide what this was all about. He told us that these people had nothing at all in life, and after having this treatment, they all then became professional beggars. I found this so disgusting and the guide told us that no westerners were allowed to see this, and I told him I wished I had not seen either.

We then flew to Madras and were taken to the factory and introduced to the management and had some sandwiches and lemonade before touring the factory, which was not very impressive.

They then took as out to their rear yard where all the packing cases that we had shipped were stacked. I saw a stack of the faschia cases and asked if they had a fork lift to lift the top case down to the floor. After crashing into the cases a few times, the driver eventually lifted the case down and I had a wrench and levered the top of the case off and a huge rat leapt out and ran away, which made me jump!. I then looked into the case and removed a panel, only to find that all that remained was the metal frame of the panel, together with the parts and the vinyl covering left. I showed the Rover team, and they could not believe it, as what had happened was that the rats had eaten into the back of the cases, and eaten all the foam inserts of the faschia.

So although the Indian company was not happy that I had found it, it was then proved that it was not the fault of our packing and so all possible charges were dropped against us by Rover. They apologised for the problem, and asked us if there was anything that we would like to do whilst were in the country, and I cheekily said that a weekend in Sri Lanka would be nice! To my amazement, they agreed, and said it would be arranged for the next day. So my manager and I flew to Columbo and was taken to a hotel on the beach, which was lovely.

We had breakfast the next day and decided to walk the beach, and suddenly a gang of young boys descended on us begging, so we gave them a few indian coins we had and they disappeared except one of boys who held our hands, then told me that he wanted to learn English, and asked us to go back to his village down the beach, which we were a bit concerned but we went. On arrival his family came out and greeted us very well and invited us into their dwelling, and proceeded to give us some snacks and drinks. They then asked us if we could take their young son back to England for a new life. I told them this was not possible, and they were very upset but understood.

We left and next day we flew back to England very relieved that we had resolved the claims.

Due to the large amount of transport required I decided to set up a new company with the owner of the Transport company and called it Avonvale Stratford Ltd.

This worked well for some years until the partner and I had a big fallout, and I decided to buy him out as a big personal package, which he agreed, and had his solicitor draw up the necessary papers.

All went well until I was in my office at Alcester and 2 guys arrived from the VAT offices.

I took them into my office and they explained that they were enquiring into the package that we agreed for my partners payout.

I said I need to talk with my wife who was in another office and picked up the phone. He slammed his hand over mine and said "no...where is she?", and we both walked to her office and Lin came down to my office.

She told them about the transaction and said all the necessary papers were in our Redditch office, so I again tried to phone and speak with the girl in accounts there, and again he slammed his hand over mine and said "we will go there".

We got outside and I said to Lin get in my car and he said "no...into mine please"

So I went with the one guy and Lin went with the other to Redditch offices, and when we got there, Mary who ran the accounts brought in all the associated paperwork, which after they went through, explained that they were happy with what they had discovered. I asked what was the problem, and they said that it was concerning non paid VAT on his part, which showed different details to the paperwork they had just been shown.

I asked what would have happened if it didn't show that and he said I would have been in Winson prison with the hour!

They thanked us profusely and said they hope we didn't get too upset, and left, much to our relief.

We later found out that he was finally caught and was sent to prison for massive non payment of VAT

Work returned to normal and we then had another enquiry from Leyland Trucks, from a friend of the assistant manager at Stratford, to ask if we would be interested in giving them a quote for receiving, dismantling and shipping part CKD, of their Leyland Road train vehicles to Australia.

We spent a week at Leyland to see how this would work, as they were currently doing this operation in-house.

They then started the contract, delivering 8 vehicles per week, as when stripped down, we could get 4 vehicles into a 40ft container.

So another contract and getting to be a very busy packing unit.

We then were asked whether we would like to quote for packing and shipping the running gear for Minimokes to Portugal, where they made their own body and upholstery and assembled the vehicle. We were again successful in obtaining the business, and so started another different part of the operation.

However we had a phone call to inform us that the Portugese factory was claiming shortages from our packing, so I asked for the appropriate paperwork to enable me to check on how this was happening.

After some extensive checking, I found that there was a pattern to their claims, which meant that after a period of

8 weeks, they had enough spare parts to assemble another vehicle, as our packing lists showed.

Again Rover told me that we would be going out to the factory to check out the claims, and I asked if I could wear a Rover inspectors overall, and that would enable me to see round the factory. They agreed to this and we set off to the site.

We spent 2 days there and I was going round the factory chatting to employees, and seeing what I could find about the problem.

One guy I saw was on the assembly line and kept going off to a store in the corner of the factory and coming back with some parts for the assembly line. I chatted to him and eventually asked to see what his store was all about.

He took me there and I was amazed to find all the parts on the claims report, together with our pack sheets, which clearly showed what parts were being claimed for.

I went back to the offices and asked for one of the Rover guys to come with me, and they were horrified to find what I had uncovered. It clearly let us off the hook, so again all our expenses were paid for and we were given a bonus payment for the inconvenience. Another problem solved!!

I decided that the family and I needed a well earned break, so I took them for a week to Majorca for a holiday. We landed in Palma and I hired a small Fiat car for the week, and we set off to the hotel.

At the first set of traffic lights, I stopped as the traffic lights were turning to red, and immediately a car hit us right up the back. I got out and asked the guy what he was doing and he told me that in Palma you don't stop until the light goes directly to red!!. Another car was sent and we again set off to the hotel, this time arriving without a problem.

We had a lovely break, and we were all somewhat revived, and whilst we were there, I looked up a friend who lived in Evesham, and had recently bought an apartment in Palma. He showed us round and told me the price which was very reasonable, and informed me that there was another similar apartment one floor up, so we arranged to have a look. It was in very good condition and so when we returned to England, I made an offer and it was accepted, and so I employed a Spanish solicitor to do the deal and obtained the keys. I went back over to sign the deal, and sent monies over to a Barclays bank, that had just opened up in Palma. The bank manager was an English guy who had just moved over to Palma to run the branch. We got on well and he said whenever I was in town to pop in and have a chat. When I next went over, I went in and asked to see him and he invited me into his office, and we had coffees and brandies, followed by more brandies and we chatted about his new position and new environment.

He turned out to be a very nice guy, and I often popped in to see him and Lin could not work out why I was so happy on my return to the apartment!!!

We had the apartment for a period of 8 ½ years and we had some very good times there. On one occasion we went to our favourite restaurant called Mario's, which was half owned by Mario and half owned by Frankie Vaughan the singer, who used to appear at xmas times and sing in the restaurant.

We knew all the waiters well and they were very good and friendly, and late into the afternoon, there was just one other table with guests on the opposite side of the restaurant, and Jesus, the waiter, suddenly moved us close to them as they said it was quiet. We got chatting to the two couples and they asked us where we were from, so I told them that we lived in England but had an apartment just down the road. They were all Spanish, and said they had come over to Palma for a break. I invited them back for a drink and they accepted so we left and they followed us back. Once in the apartment

I said to one of the guys..."Please pour yourselves a drink of wine from the small wine rack, whilst I serve your wives a drink". He picked out several bottles and said "Crap, Crap", and I thought that I am not going to like you, but then found a bottle and said "Ah not bad"

We all sat down and I asked them where they lived and he said in Barcelona, and gave me his business card which showed me that he was the managing director of Rioja wines, and also a director of Barcelona football club.

After some time, he asked me what I was doing the following weekend, and I said we were there for another 6 days, so he invited me over to Barcelona to watch a football game, and he would get me the tickets for the flights.

I asked Lin and she said she was ok as she had our friends there until we returned home, so I was free to go. The tickets arrived and off I went on the Saturday morning, to be greeted at the airport and taken to the club. We went straight to the directors box where I was wined and dined and enjoyed a great game of football. I then flew back to Palma and rejoined my wife and friends.

On the one day morning there was a knock on the door and I opened it to find a delivery driver who asked me if I was Senor Hughes, and then gave me a box.

This contained some of the finest Rioja wines and a note asking me to replace the wines in my rack!!! What an experience.

After the 8 ½ years we decided that it was time to move on and so sell the apartment. I phoned my solicitor and told him about the sale and he advised me to get the services of a female estate agent who apparently was very good, and I managed to get her to set the ball rolling.

She phoned me about 3 weeks later and said she had 2 customers interested in the property, and said she would keep me informed. The following week, I was told that one had dropped out but the other was very interested, and was going to make an offer. I had inflated the price anyway so when he offered me just under the price I accepted, and so she went ahead with the deal, and told me that I would need to go over to clinch the deal.

Another two weeks went by and I had a call to inform me that it was all set and ready to go, with a meeting at the Notary in Palma, so I flew over and stayed in the apartment ready for the next day's meeting.

The purchaser was from mainland Spain and had a convalescent home in Palma, so it was ideal for him to be close whenever he needed to be there.

He was accompanied by 3 bank managers, his solicitor and I had my agent and solicitor there too. The Notary commenced the meeting stating the reason for being there and assuring that all the people required were present.

He then asked the purchaser for the agreed figure and he then had his three bank managers to produce the appropriate cheques, which he then checked and stated that it was short of the total amount. The purchaser then produced a shopping bag with the equivalent of £10,000 in notes which then totaled to the correct amount.

With that the Notary left the room, as this was classified as "black money", which was to deflate the true price and to pay "black money", to avoid them paying tax on the true amount. The cheques and shopping bag was handed to my solicitor and he checked to see that the correct amount was all there. He then left, and my agent started chatting to the purchaser and he stated that I could stay in the apartment until Saturday, the day of my flight, on the proviso that I played a game with him. I said he had been playing a game with me for a week and she then told me it was a game of Chino, which I was then told was a game played with three coins in the hand...Spoof to me!!!

We left the office and sat downstairs on a bar front in deckchairs and we started to play the best of five games, if I won I stayed, and if I lost I moved out.

The first game he won, the second I won, the third he won and the fourth game I won so it was all on the last game. It was my call and I called loudly..."Spoof", which to the unannounced means nil.

He then stood up and shouted " Bastido", which meant that I was staying in the apartment!! I proudly left with my bag of black money.

On the Saturday morning of my flight, there was a knock on the door, and the purchaser arrived with a bottle of whisky, and said that it had been a pleasure to do business with me, and we cracked the bottle open and had a few enjoyable drinks, and he turned out to be quite a decent guy.

He asked me why the garage down below the apartment had been not in the sale, and I said it had a separate Escitura, so I would sell that separately through my agent, and if he wanted, he could bid for that with her.

I purchased the Escitura years before and for a price of approximately £1000, and so it was left with my agent to sell for me.

She called me a few weeks later and told me that she had an offer of almost £7000, so I hastily agreed and the sale was set up, and she phoned a few days later to say that I was to go over and sign the deal. The reason for the big increase was due to the fact of the big parking shortage in Palma

I invited a couple of friends, one of which was Alan Towers the midlands TV presenter, who was a good friend, and also another guy who wanted to look at some property over there.

We flew over and I collected the money, and we went out for a slap up meal, back to the hotel before flying home the next day.

Chapter 3

THE CANCER

The Rover SD1 contract was slowing down, and I was told that we only had another three months to run on the contract as India was working on their own production vehicle, however there was another contract in the offing.

This was a reciprocal trading arrangement between Rover and Honda Japan, in which Rover shipped the Triumph Acclaim to Japan and they shipped the Honda Acclaim to England.

So, we had about 2 months of learning about the operation and then we secured the contract.

It was a bit messy to start with as were running out the SD1 contract and commencing the Acclaim contract. However, after a rocky start it settled down into a routine CKD packing mode.

We had a visitation from the Honda Japan company who saw how we packed and shipped the vehicles to them, and Rover suggested that we ought to visit the Honda factory to see how they packed and shipped.

So, this visit was arranged and I flew out to Japan with the Rover guys first class on JAL, landing in Tokyo. AS we were the only passengers in first class one of the air stewardesses handed me a carrier bag with three bottles of wine and said enjoy. We then had a taxi to the hotel Otani, where I checked in and was given the keys to my room on the 22nd floor. They told me the lifts were straight opposite the entrance, so I get in the lift and pressed the 22 key.

The lift then set off and for the first four floors the lift was inside the building and then it went outside and climbed up the outside of the building, which was quite an experience as the lift had glass walls and glass floor.

The next morning we met for breakfast and then took a taxi to Shinjuku station the catch the train to the Honda factory. This was so busy with little Japanese running along the station platforms, and I was told that a million people pass through the station every day

We had been told that you had to time the trip which was 28 minutes and 23 seconds, and we wondered why this was, but soon found out that for the first 4 stops the stations were in Japanese and English but in Japanese only after that.

So after exactly the time, the train stopped, the doors opened and two white lines on the platform indicated where you stepped out, to be greeted by 2 Honda guys bowing and saying good morning.

They drove us to the Honda factory, which was very interesting.

After introductions all round we were shown round the factory, where we spent most of the day seeing how their operation worked. I could not believe the cleanliness of the site and how the workforce was applying their skills on the production line, especially after seeing how the Rover plant in Longbridge operated!!

We were shown their CKD operation which was different to ours, as there is not much timber in Japan, so all the cases containing the parts were made of metal, whereas ours were in timber. This proved to be a little bonus to us when the contract commenced, as we were able to crush the containers and sell the scrap metal!

Eventually late afternoon, the workforce started to leave the production lines and I asked what was happening, and was told they then all then go to the restaurant areas, to discuss their day's work and see how they can improve for tomorrow.

A little different to Longbridge, where if you stood there at clocking out time, you would get killed in the rush!!

We spent three days with Honda and before we left, I managed to get a few hours to look around Tokyo town, and get some little gifts for the wife and family.

One was a pen type item, which if you pressed the top it would scan a page, and then you could download it into your PC. I had never seen this before. Another was a small radio with a small TV screen mounted inside and gave a very good picture.

We then flew back from Narita airport and arrived back in England after a very enlightening trip.

The contract commenced and went very well, and lasted for 2 years, before slowing down and finished.

Back at the works, I had a phone call to inform me that Robert, the original guy I worked for had died, which was nothing to do with the pins my wife had been sticking in an effigy of him for ever!!

I was told by the police that they knew he had organised my break in, and were just about to charge him but he died before they could get him.

I then had an enquiry from NSS newsagents who wanted to have a warehouse to receive and store items, that they then sent out to all their stores for promotional sales every month.

This was a really different type operation to what we had done and so we looked at the specification and quoted and they awarded us the contract.

This meant that I had to rent another warehouse for a period of 2 years, which was the time the contract was to run.

It was a stop start type operation, as we were receiving parts for a month and then picking, packing and shipping for the end of the month.

This went well and although it was sometimes a problem to get the suppliers to deliver to us on time, we managed to complete the contract.

I then had a phone call from another contract packaging company who wanted to know if we were interested in selling out to them, so we held various meetings with them and finally agreed a sale, and they requested that I was retained as Commercial Director.

This meant that I had to travel to Rugby every day which was a change from my usual 15 minutes journey to the works.

All of the packing contracts were then transferred to Rugby and worked in league with the team there to get things moving efficiently.

I had to install a new computer system to handle the Unipart and Landrover business, and I advertised for this position, and found a young guy who had recently moved from Zimbabwe, and used to run the computer system for Rio Tinto Mines.

He started with me and I told him what I needed and he wrote the software and very soon we had the system up and running, to handle the various contracts.

My wife also moved over to the Rugby site and was working in the accounts department.

After about a year I was offered a Wellman check by my local doctor, and I thought I would take this offer, so I went to see him and he gave me a thorough check and said I will phone you and let you know the results.

He phoned me the next day and said he wanted me to go to see a specialist oncologist in Edgbaston that evening, and when I asked why, he told me that he was worried about my prostate.

I went and saw the guy, and he did some checks and then told me he wanted me back the next day to do some more.

I arrived and he told me that he was going to do a biopsy of my prostate, which he did and removed 13 pieces for investigation

He then phoned the next day and said I need to see you this evening, so along I went again, and I took Lin with me as I was very worried.

He told me that I had quite severe prostate cancer and he would need to operate, and remove the prostate. I said but what are the options, and he said there are none. I said sorry I don't work like that, I need to know more, and said I would contact him .

I then sat in the car with Lin and cried and said where do we go from here?

The next day I went on to the PC and trolled the world looking for alternative treatments.

The best thing I found after contacting people all over the world, was a treatment called Brachytherapy, and when I checked for this in the UK, I found that a surgeon in Leeds had just started this type of treatment, but he had only done 78 so far, so I was a bit wary of this. More time on the PC, and then managed to find 2 English guys who had severe prostate cancer and went to the USA for this Brachytherapy treatment, and would you believe that they both lived within ½ hour from where I lived.

They both invited me over to explain where and what this was all about, and it turned out that they had been to the Dattoli Cancer Centre in Sarasota, Florida for their treatment, and I could ask whatever I liked, and they would give me the answers. They both had the all clear after their treatments, so I was very impressed, and thanked them profusely, and decided to contact Doctor Dattoli the next day.

I spoke to the Centre and he was busy giving treatment and I was told he would ring me back, which he did that evening at about 8 o'clock English time.

I told him about my situation and he asked me to e mail him all the results that I had, which I did, and he again phoned me to say that he could help me.

I then contacted the Oncologist I had seen and told him that I was going to have Brachytherapy treatment in the USA, and he said "On your own head be it"!!

I then started to research along with the centre, who were very helpful, and even gave me some contacts, who rented out their properties for cancer patients as they had family members at the Dattoli centre and would help in this direction if needed. I managed to contact one elderly couple, who said we could rent her mother's bungalow, as she had died of cancer, and they offered this property to help other cancer patients.

I then confirmed a date for the treatment, and also for the bungalow, and Lin and I booked the flights to Tampa, in Florida.

We arrived in Tampa, and as it was just after the 9/11 disaster, the security was very strict. They took me on one side and asked what all the items were with me which was a laptop and printer as well as other items, so they made me stand on one side to frisk me, and stripped me down to my underpants, whilst everyone was passing by. I shouted to Lin to look after our cases, but I was held there for about ¾ hour, until they were happy to let me go. Jobs for the boys!!

We arrived at Tampa to be collected by the couple, and drive back to their bungalow in a small village called

Nokomis, which was about 10 miles from Sarasota, so just ideal.

They helped us settle in and then told us we must be outside the bungalow at 4.30 that afternoon and they would join us. I wondered what this was about, but just before 4.30 they arrived and told us to look East and we would be able to see the launch of the Columbus spacecraft. We could clearly see the rocket take off from the Kennedy space centre, and the trail of smoke it left behind, so quite an eventful day.

The husband of the couple, Royce, was a lovely guy and drove us around to show us where places were, including the Cancer centre, so I could get my bearings.

I told him that I wanted to rent a car, and he said why don't you buy one as you are here for about 13 weeks, and he knew a good second hand car sales guy, so he took me there and I managed to buy a small Chevvy, which did the job for us.

My treatment was to start 2 days away, so we got everything ready for the trip into Sarasota.

We arrived at the centre, and booked in, and then we both met Dr Dattoli and his accomplice, who then showed us round and told us how they would proceed. The first thing to be done was to set me up in the Radiotherapy room, as they needed to make plaster casts for my feet whilst on the table, so I lay down and they told me I must always wear the same shoes for treatment, and they measured me up and the next day I was fitted into them. The idea was that they needed me to be in exactly the same position every time I was there.

They also checked all my PSA details and the letter I had taken from the English Oncologist.

So I was now ready for the start, but before that we had to attend a meeting they called "Beamers ", due to the fact that we were all having radiotherapy treatment with beams to our bodies.

I had to stand up and state that my name was Reg Hughes from England, and I had just arrived to commence my treatment. All the other patients clapped and I sat down and then others did the same thing. We had to attend this meeting every Thursday evening to explain where we were with the treatment and how it was going.

So the next day I was told that I must drink half a litre of water just before my treatment, and so whilst I was driving into Sarasota, Lin was helping me drink from a bottle so that I was ready when we got there.

I left Lin in the waiting room, and was taken to the radiotherapy room where I was told all about the procedure and how many sessions I would have and then finally I would go to the Sarasota main hospital for the Brachytherapy.

I then had tattoos on my left and right side of my stomach, which was to make sure that they could line me up with my feet in the casts, and the rays lined up to the tattoos. The half litre of water was to make sure that the bladder was away from the prostate, so they could make direct contact with it.

When the machine started up I was gradually turned round in all directions for about 40 minutes, and then during that, I could watch what they were doing on a screen above me, and see where the rays were hitting my prostate.

This was the same treatment I had every week for 12 weeks, and then they said I was ready for the Brachytherapy, which meant that they would insert 65 radioactive seeds directly into my prostate, which would kill the cancer along with the radiotherapy from the inside.

The date was set for the 23rd January 2003 and we had to leave for Sarasota hospital at 4.30 in the morning.

The lead up was quite a feat too, with hard fast instructions to get the system completely cleared out prior to going in to hospital. I could have nothing else to eat or drink after 3.00pm, unless it was clear liquid. The first thing was to drink a bottle of Magnesium Citrate at 6.00pm in the evening (now referred to as the "depth charge"), which starts to clear from the top down, then later that evening 2 enemas, to be followed by 2 more in the morning, so as we had to leave home at 4.30am, it meant an early start and several hasty dashes to the bathroom.

It was like a Blaster Bates scene..."it was when the depth charge going down met the enemas coming up"!!

Lin decided that we need to be up at about 2.30am, to enable all the things to get finished in time, so the alarm was set and not much sleep that evening.

We left home at 4.45am, drove to the hospital, where a young lad greeted us and took charge of the car, parking it for us until we were ready to leave...a bit different to UK. We were then taken to a pre-op room where I was got ready, and felt like a trussed up chicken, in gown and slippers. Dr Dattoli arrived about 7.15am and spent some time explaining the complete procedure to us both...I didn't really want to know all the sordid details, just wanted to get on with it, but saying that, he is very thorough and left about 7.45am.

They wheeled me down to the part of the operating theatre, which is specially kitted out for all the Dattoli seeding, and then an anesthetist gave me the epidural in the lower back, and also a sleepy type drug, which did soon make me feel very drowsy, but I could still see all the computers and sophisticated gear being made ready. My legs were put into stirrups, and I could just about make out that they belonged to me! (They said that all the wives had commented on this part, saying that it was payback time!!..what a comment!!). They then put a curtain up between my knees and all the team of guys working behind, but I could still hear what was going on for a short time, before I finally drifted off into oblivion.

Dr Dattoli had explained that when they use the colour Doppler camera at that point I was completely relaxed, unlike on previous times, and they then get the true position of the prostate, which they need for the implants. Although they have made a plan of how and where they will place the seeds, they finalise the job at that point, and then it is like a game of "Battleships"...ie. place a grid type template and then put needles through the grid in A1 , D5, G13 etc, which place the seeds in the correct position. The seeds are similar to a pencil lead thickness and about 1/4 inch long and are made from Palladium 103, and very expensive, and are made to order 2 days before the treatment, delivered to the hospital the evening before the operation. The seeds start to discharge radiation immediately, and deliver half the dose in the first 17 days, and it takes approximately 3-4 months for all of the radioactivity to be delivered.

During the implant process, one guy is logging the seed placement closely and Dr Dattoli is making the decision of where he would place the next one, and is also listening to the blood flow in the prostate, and as he explained, cancer cells need more blood to survive on, and so he can tell by listening, exactly where to place the seeds in conjunction with the model they had already prepared. He actually said that he had put 3 or 4 more in at the last minute, but wasn't sure they would stay. As it happened I did lose 4 when I first had a pee next day!, but as he had used 65 seeds, he wasn't too concerned and said it would not detract from the overall effect.

I was then wheeled back to the recovery room for about an hour, and was moved from there after I could wiggle my toes, so on to the private room where Lin was waiting with baited breath, and I had to assure her that I was OK, but by this time I had a catheter, and also an intravenous drip, so leads and things everywhere, and obviously no feeling in the lower part of my body. The hospital staff, which are also trained with the Dattoli techniques, are superb and very attentive, making sure that we both had everything we needed in the way of food, drinks and for Lin the sleeping arrangements in the form of a bed settee, which was only pointed out after Lin had snuggled down in the settee!!

We both slept very little, as you know what it is like, the hourly checking of blood pressures, refilling the drips, pills, and all the other things they need to do to ensure that everything's OK. Then at 3.15am they said it was time to get all the tubes out and settle me down for getting ready, so another tear raising with the catheter removal , and I certainly was pleased it was all over. Breakfast arrived at 7.30 and after that I was passed fit to get a shower which felt wonderful, and told that I could not go until I had proved that I could pee without problems, and that was when we discovered the 4 seeds, oh well at least they didn't want to put them back!!...so a total of 61 still in place.

I managed the feat without too much effort, then Dr Dattoli said that I was cleared to go, and could even play golf that same day if I wished. I said that would be wonderful, because I could not play before!!

I was then wheeled down in a chair to the exit, where the valet parking lad delivered my car to us, and away we drove to the Dattoli centre to get a CT scan and X rays, but when we got there, we found that the machine was down, and they were waiting for the technicians to arrive to fix it, so we were asked if they could ring us when it was up and running again, That wasn't a problem to us, but there were 2 other guys that had been done as well, and they had both planned to travel back home to various parts of the US, so they had to quickly change their plans!!. One of these guys was a Philippine, who lived north of Tampa, but had his radiation treatment in October, followed by a triple heart bypass in November, and then came back for this seeding !!!... quite a guy and he did look very fit too!!

We were all the given a "goodie" bag consisting of a mug, a keyring with seeds encased in it, a tee shirt and a pair of boxer shorts with yellow and black skull and crossbones radiation symbols all over them. We all decided that when we go back for the last radiation sessions in April, we are going to meet up and parade in the reception area in the boxer shorts..quite a sight I would think!. I had to go back for 5 more sessions of radiation, which Dattoli have now decided to add to the treatment as they need to do 2 strips of the lymph nodes...one each side of the body, to ensure complete clearance of cancer cells.

We then went shopping and before we got home as we had to buy some more drugs prescribed by Dattoli, which I have to be on for up to 3 months in some cases, another big expense, ... I shall be glad to get home and get them free on the NHS!!. ....and I have now created a speadsheet to control how and when I take them, carefully checked by Lin, as it is so complicated!

Well enough of that, the weather here has been getting colder over the last few days as a cold front is moving south from the main US, and when we got back home we couldn't believe the sight we saw in the garden. The fruit trees were covered in long icicles about 12 to 18 inches long and smothered the orange, lemon and grapefruit, ...welcome to sunny Florida!!!

So we are now on countdown to our return journey, and I must say that it will be great to get back to our own house, it does seem an eternity now since we arrived here.

One more thing we had to do was to go to the Beamers evening and tell how we had finished with the treatment, so I stood up and explained that we had finished and were going home the next day.

After that, on guy stood up and said "My name is Joe and I have finished my treatment and I am proud to say that I had my first ejaculation today", then sat down, to which his wife stood up and clapped!!

We went to a restaurant situated on Venice airport and as we drove there I noticed that a small bungalow which was empty, had a huge American flag on a pole towering way above the bungalow and didn't know why.

When I asked Royce about it he explained that it was there because two of the men who bombed 9/11 lived there, and had been trained to fly at Venice airport, and the strange thing was that all they were interested in really was how to take off, no-one thought any more of it until after 9/11 !!

During the time we spent in Florida, we managed to travel about and covered some 5000 miles around the state, and then managed to sell the car back to the dealer for slightly more than I paid for it, so a great result.

Royce and Evelyn then drove us back to Tampa airport, where we said our goodbyes, and thanked them for their kind friendship, and we are still in touch with them today.

As we waited for take off , they announced that the Columbia spaceship had blown up on return to earth, so we saw them take off on arrival in Florida, and sadly that had happened on the day of our return.

Dr Dattoli wanted me to go back every year for a check up, so we did this for a further 4 years, renting a villa and spending a few days holiday there as well.

Another year when I went back for my annual checkup we took my daughter Karen, her husband Rick and the two boys Jake and Luke aged 4 and 6.

We took them to Disneyland in Orlando where we all enjoyed the day, and the boys really enjoying all the rides

Rick decided to have a trip in a cage and be lowered down into a pool, with sharks swimming all round him. Jake could see him in the cage from behind glass walls of the pools.

He very proudly shouted to passers by..."That's my dad in there" !!

I had to have some blood tests, and various checks, and then the final check was to sit in a high chair with my legs wide apart and in stirrups, and then a camera would be inserted to check on the prostate. Lin was sitting by my side watching this all happen on a large screen, and could see the camera moving, and even hear the bloodflow, as it pumped round.

Mike the camera operator was a nice guy and the second year I went, he told me that he had a new piece of equipment, and when I asked what it was he told me that he had a new camera, which was 3 mm less in diameter, which did make things a bit easier for me!!

The last year we went, my good friend Alan Towers asked me if he and his wife could come with us and I told him that we had rented the villa and so if he got his flights it would be ok.

We spent 5 days in Sarasota, and had some good tours round, and some nice meals out. We were in one restaurant one evening, and when we had finished the meal, we had ½ a bottle of red wine left, so Alan called the waiter over and asked him to put the top back on so we could take it with us. He replied " No sir can't do that....this is a brown bag state".... apparently you cannot take booze out unless it is in a brown bag anywhere.

Alan stood up to his full height, and said "You mean to tell me that I cannot take a bottle of wine from here , but you can go and f-----ng bomb Iraq.

The waiter replied "Yes sir...life's a sh-t aint it", and gave us the bottle and wished us goodnight!!

Chapter 4

DIVE BOAT TRIP TO THE RED SEA

Whilst we were dealing with Unipart, my friend the Purchase Director phoned me and said that his manager had been sent to Bologna to help set up a new Unipart parts operation there, and he had been there for 14 weeks and was missing the UK, so he asked me if I would like to go and visit him, and I would go as a Unipart Inspector!!

I said what a good idea, I would love to go, so we flew to Pisa airport where Nigel his manager picked us up in a Rover Princess 1800, and took us to the leaning tower of Pisa to see it, and then started the return journey to Bologna, stopping at a few alehouses on the way, finally arriving in the town.

As we stopped at an island Nigel pulled out the wrong way and an Innocenti mini hit us amidships, and the impact broke my rear window and threw me out of the car, with me finishing up lying in the middle of the Road.

John the Purchase Director told Nigel to clear off quickly from the scene, and an ambulance arrived and they lifted me into it, only to be pulled out by John and we set off to the hotel we had been booked in. The police arrived later and no-one knew what had happened, but Nigel did get charged later.

However when we arrived back at the hotel, I was quite bruised and battered and sore, and we went to the bar to have a drink, only to find Nigel sitting there enjoying more drinks.

I was a bit better then next morning and we had breakfast and then Nigel sorted another car and drove us into the new parts depot, and showed us round.

He then suggested we get lunch at a small Italian restaurant that he had found and was very friendly with the owner and his wife.

We were introduced and had a lovely lunch served by both him and his very large wife, who did their utmost to make us very welcome.

After lunch he then suggested that we might like to try some of his Grappa, and so we started to try all his big range of Grappa, lasting about 2 hours.

We left and went back to the hotel and got some sleep. The next morning I was so ill and could not stop throwing up, and on the way to the depot, they had to stop the car for me to be ill. I have never ever touched any Grappa again!!

Nigel was then going back to England the next day and we flew back the day after to be picked up at Heathrow by Nigel in the same princess 1800 that we had the accident in. I was not thrilled to do that but it got us back to Oxford where I left for home after an interesting and wearing trip!!

In 1980 I was having a drink with my best friend Joe Turner, and he told me that he and his brother Tony had 3 dive boats that were operating out of Eilat, and two of the boats need some refit work doing on them, so they were to be sailing to Athens to have the work done on them.

He thought it would be a good idea if he and his wife Barbara, and Lin and myself joined the boat (Lady Jenny 5) there and made the trip back to Eilat.

He checked to see when this would be possible, and so we made all the necessary arrangements to fly to Athens, stay in a hotel and join the boat the next day.

We flew to Athens, but the flight was delayed, and so we arrived there late at night and after hiring a car, we arrived at the hotel at about 1.30 in the morning, and checked in.

In the morning, we had breakfast and went to check out and the manager said we must pay for the two nights that we had booked, but we told him that things had changed and we only had the one night. So we only paid for one night, and he got very angry. Joe told me to get the girls and the cases as we were leaving quickly.

We left the hotel, with the manager screaming at us that he was going to call the police, but we kept going, on the lookout for police cars!!

We then had to find the boat which Joe told me was in Piraeus harbour, which we eventually found, and scoured the harbour but could not find the boat. We found the harbourmaster, who told us that it was not there and told us where it was moored. When we eventually found the boat it was moored almost opposite the hotel we had stayed in !!

We unloaded our cases and went on to the boat and met the crew:-

Mark the Captain, Cliff the chef, Eric the Engineer and Dominick the Steward.

So there were four of us and four of them on a 75 foot boat, which seemed ideal.

We stowed all our things on board, and Joe said he had to go into town to collect some items, and set off on a scooter which was on board. He asked me if I could help sort a delivery of drinks, which was due to arrive shortly.

A 7.5 ton vehicle arrived loaded with booze, which was to be unloaded and stowed in the boat, which was for all the guests that would be using the boat whilst it was in Eilat, which would be for the next 9 months.

I helped unload and it took us 2 hours to get all the booze on board, and Joe arrived back and I said you just timed that right!!

We settled into the boat and the crew told us the plans for the trip, as it was due to start the next day, by sailing across the Mediterranean to Port Said, the start of the Suez canal.

The weather was wonderful, and so we were well looked after by the crew, and enjoying nice meals cooked by the chef, and drinking some of the booze that I had unloaded, and enjoying the sunshine on the top deck.

Joe and I managed to find some fishing rods, and we enjoyed a few hours fishing and caught some small Dorado and other colourful fish, which Cliff the chef cooked for us.

On arrival at Port Said, we moored up in the harbour as we were not due to leave until morning. As we sat on deck enjoying the sunshine some "bum" boats circled us and were begging for anything they could get. One dark Egyptian stood up and pointed to Lin and said" Hi, you are a wee smasher", in a broad Scottish accent, which was most out of place!!

The harbourmaster then arrived with what looked like a rolled up newspaper under his arm, came on board and made the arrangements for the pilots, but on condition that we gave him a bottle of whisky, which, would you believe just fitted into this rolled up newspaper, which turned out to be a nice cylindrical tube, just right to take a bottle!!

He then left and the skipper then got the pilot on board with us, and we had to follow an allocated boat through the canal, so this Egyptian came on board, and he told us the plan, and the first thing he wanted was to ask what we had for him.

We gave him some pens, toothpaste and a bottle of whisky, which seemed to sort him out.

At the allocated time we moved into position in the canal, only to find that the boat we were to follow was a munitions boat, which didn't go down too well with me!!

Anyway off we set, down the canal, and were due to change pilots when we arrived at the Bitter lakes , which was well down towards the bottom of the canal.

When we got there, the pilot said he was leaving, but Joe said to me to keep him there until the other pilot got on board, so I had to restrain him, as if he left, we could be made to pay for another pilot.

Eventually the other pilot arrived and I let him go and he left the boat.

The new pilot then asked us what we had for him, so again we had to sort some items, including whisky, for him. We set off again and when we arrived at the start of the Red Sea, he left us and so were now on our own completely.

We sailed into the Red Sea, and then turned left into the Straits of Tirran, which was to lead us up the Gulf of Aquaba and then onwards to Eilat.

The weather was wonderful, and I was watching all the shipwrecks lined up on the reefs lining the sides of the gulf. I could not believe how many and there were also smaller boats with people on, who appeared to be taking whatever they could find from the wrecks.

We had our evening meal on board deck, and then settled down in the galley for a few drinks before retiring to bed.

The next morning we got up and looked out and the weather had changed completely, and it was pouring down with rain and the wind was starting to blow very hard. I asked the skipper what the forecast was and he said it is not looking good. One hour later and we were into the middle of a force 10 gale and the wind was howling and throwing us all over the place.

The skipper then told us that we were past the point of no return, and to keep on track he started to zigzag up the gulf, which was apparently the only way he could keep control of the boat. This weather went on all day and into the night, and whilst we were pushing on, we could see very large oil tankers heading straight down the idle of the gulf, passing us within what seemed like yards away.

Lin and Joe said they were going down below to their cabins, but I couldn't do that, and so Barbara and I sat in the galley drinking and wishing the storm to be gone. I went up to the wheelhouse and spoke to the skipper, who looked very scared, and asked him how we were doing, and he replied that he thought we might make it ok. He had been too occupied controlling the boat and had not had any food, so I said I would make him a sandwich, so down to the galley and I had a job opening the fridge, and preparing his food.

I managed to struggle back up to the wheelhouse, and then saw a huge green wave hit the front windscreen of the boat, followed by another huge wave, which crashed onto the front deck, and ripped off one of the new dive tanks that had been fitted, and tossed it over the side.

I was really scared then and went back down to the galley and made sure that Barbara was secure, and grabbed a bottle of whisky and left for the rear of the boat where there was a nice big seat, which I strapped myself into, and helped myself to a large measure and thought .."if I am going down to Davey Jones locker I might as well get drunk "

The next thing I remember was waking up and finding that the sun had come out and it was flat calm, and Joe was shouting " Hughsie….come and help me", as he had caught a big Lampouki fish.

I got myself together and went to the front of the boat where Joe was struggling to land the fish. I went up to him and cut the line, leaving the fish to glide away.

He asked me what the hell did I do that for and I replied that we had managed to escape the storm, so why not let him go. After a brief shouting episode, he calmed down and we all went and sat in the galley and had some breakfast, served by the chef and steward.

We were about 5 hours from Eilat, and so we relaxed and enjoyed the last part of our journey as we got closer, we noticed a fast boat coming towards us, and as they got close I could see that there were guys in uniforms with rifles on their shoulders. They called out for us to pull over and then 2 guys dropped into the water and dived under the boat, apparently to ensure that we had not any mines underneath the boat, and then proceeded to climb on deck and ask for our passports, which they then kept until we left Eilat. They then went right through the boat, checking on everything, and one soldier, who was about 6ft 5ins stood by me holding his rifle, and he was wearing a hairnet to keep his long hair in place. Lin whispered to me I bet you daren't tell him to take it off, and I told her to shut up quickly.

After all the checks, they allowed us to moor up in the harbour, and we settled down and thanked the crew for their help and good work to get us there in one piece, and told them that we would take them all out for a meal that evening.

We found a nice restaurant, and had a very pleasant meal with them, and said we would head off back to the boat, but the crew said that they were staying and going out on the town, so we left them to it.

We got back to the boat, and settled down in the galley with some nice wine and recapped about our journey.

Joe and Barbara then had a fall out over something trivial, and Lin said she was going to make some coffee, if anyone wanted some.

She came back and said to Joe that we were going to bed and would he just check the cooker as she could thought that she had not turned the gas off.

We went to bed and slept very well, and next morning Lin got up early, and went down to make a cup of tea for us both. She had on a very flimsy nightie, and a pair of panties, and she smoked too in those days.

When she got to the galley, she lit a cigarette, and there was one big bang, and she came screaming out crying.

I went out and found that she had blown the pilot light out on the gas, and it had been leaking gas all night, and Joe forgot to check it.

Back to Lin and I found that the blast had shredded her nightie and panties and burnt all her stomach and ripped some of her pubes off.

Dominic the steward said he would help, so we got her into the bath and tried to soothe her with cold water, but it made her scream, and we knew that we needed to get medical attention, so I shot off into town, and got a chemist to come and offer his help, bringing some cream to apply on her tummy, and that did start to ease the problem. We were very lucky that the whole boat did not blow up, and kill us all!!

Lin spent a very uncomfortable night on the boat, and the next morning we had breakfast and thanked the crew and said our goodbyes, and after hiring a car we set off on the long journey to Jerusalem. I was the nominated driver and so we settled Lin in the car and made her as comfortable as possible and, set off.

We had to go through a few "Checkpoint Charlies", which consisted of a staggered road system, with soldiers with machine guns, who made us all get out of the car, whilst they checked inside, and also checked our passports. It was a bit scary, but we finally entered the outskirts of Jerusalem, and found a small restaurant where we parked and went in for a bite to eat.

We were all dressed quite modestly, but Barbara had a pair of shorts on with a brief top, and she had some very harsh looks as we walked around the town. She did stand out from the rest of the people and I was glad to get back in the car and head off.

We then headed for Tel Aviv, where we were due to get a flight back to London. We arrived at the airport, and checked in and handed our cases in as usual. When we were then called to board the plane, we had to go out on the tarmac by the plane, where all the cases were lined up, and we had to identify our own cases, which were then loaded into the hold, before we could board the plane.

We arrived safely at Heathrow, where we checked into a hotel for the night before travelling back to the midlands. We had a meal in the restaurant, and went to our rooms, quite weary, and Lin was still suffering with her burns.

I switched on the TV, and thought there was a film on but then realised that it was the news, and it then gave details all about the siege of the Iranian Embassy, which was happening live.

I helped Lin to bed and sat with a glass of whisky recounting the amazing trip we had just completed, and it all happened in 10 days!!......A trip never to forget.

Chapter 5

DAUGHTER KAREN'S WEDDING

We had a contract to manufacture the insert trays for some of the Waddington's games.

This was done on a vacuum forming machine, and the trays were formed from a base tool fixed in the machine, with a roll of film feeding over the tool.

I had to go to Waddingtons in Leeds, to discuss any new insert tray, with their engineers, who designed new games for them.

They would say that we want this that way, and I would say that it was not possible, but it could be done like this, and eventually we would agree on the layout they wanted.

I would then take that away and have a wooden sample forming tool made, and produce some samples, take them to Leeds, where they would agree, or might say that they wanted it altered slightly. This would happen until it finally ended up with the insert tray they were happy with.

The next problem was to get the colour to exactly the colour they wanted, so they gave me a pantone reference, which I had to work with.

I purchased the vacuum forming film from a company in Switzerland, so I would give them the colour reference, and then they would produce the film accordingly. The only problem is that when the heat is applied to the film in the machine it changes the colour slightly, so this has to be accounted for, but their development engineers were very good, and usually they managed to get it right first time.

I was called for a meeting in Leeds to discuss a new tray they wanted, which was a promotional deal they had done with Cadbury's, and so we managed to agree the layout for the tool, and then I had to get the Swiss company to arrange to produce the correct mauve Cadbury's colour.

This was all to happen and for me to get them samples of the tray for a toy fair which was to be held in Nuremburg. We were on a strict timeframe, and had to ensure that the trays were available for them to take with them for their stand there.

We had some problems, which delayed the programme, but eventually we produced the samples, but as they had already gone to Nuremburg, I had to fly out with the samples. I flew to Frankfurt, and then transferred to a smaller plane onward to Nuremburg.

As we approached the airport, the Pilot announced that we had a problem and he was going to make some runs over the airport to check if the undercarriage was down or not. I looked out the window and saw fire engines and other vehicles on the runway and didn't feel very happy.

The guy next to me was a Padre, and he crossed his chest and prayed, and that made me more nervous, but eventually the Pilot announced that the undercarriage was down and we could land safely.

I then had to get a taxi and rush to the toy fair and hand over the samples to the Waddington's team on their stand, and I was pleased that they all approved the samples, and thanked me very much for my efforts.

They then invited me out that evening for a slap up meal which went down very well, and I stayed the night with them and left to fly home the next morning.

My daughter Karen was working in the sales department, and said that she had received a phone call from Wilkinson Sword who were looking to contract out packing of 100, 000 razors, for a promotional Xmas programme, so she arranged for us to go to see them at their offices.

I was chatting with my Friend Joe's brother Tony, and he said that he had to go in that direction, and as he had his own plane, he offered to fly us up to Sheffield.

We met at his house in Alcester, and climbed into the plane with Karen sitting in the back seat, and I was sitting next to Tony. We set off and the weather was quite good but when we had done about half the journey, the weather closed in and it was very foggy, and I could not see much out of the windows. Tony was a qualified pilot, so he flew on instruments, and when we approached the small airport, he tuned in to speak with them, and they said that they would talk us in, as they could not see us.

Tony was working with them and as we got close he asked me to look for the white lines on the runway, and my eyes were almost popping out of my head, and suddenly I shouted "White lines", and we were about 5 yards off the line of white on the runway.

We had the meeting at Wilkinsons, and left them with a quote which they said they would come back to me the next day, and returned to the airport to fly back to Alcester. By then the weather had cleared, so it was a much more enjoyable flight back home.

Another time, I was talking with Tony, and said that we had been working long hours of late, and needs a weekend break, but didn't know where to go.

He suggested that he had a cottage down in St Ives which was not being used at the moment, so he offered it to us for the weekend.

He said that he had to go down too, as he had some business to attend to, and so I thanked him and said we would meet him on Friday for the flight.

I only told Lin about the cottage, as Lin was not good flying, so I told her that we would leave on Friday, but I had to go to the works first to drop off some keys, and as the works were close to Tony's runway, I pulled up and there in front of us was Tony's Beechcraft Bonanza plane.

She said what is going on and I told her that we were flying down in that plane. She said " I am not going in a balsa wood glider", but we managed to get her into the plane and Tony started off down the runway and then lifted up into the heavens.

She calmed down a bit as it was very clear, and such a good flight, and as we approached St Ives, I asked Tony where his cottage was in relation to the harbour, so he dipped the wings, and dived down towards the harbour pointing out the cottage. Lin was screaming in the back, telling Tony to put the plane straight.

He eased the plane level again and we landed on the golf course which was about 10 minutes from his cottage, and Tony took us and showed us round, and said he would be down on sunday afternoon to collect us and fly us back.

Lin told me she was not going back in that plane, but I said we have no other means to get back, so that was it.

He duly arrived and we flew back to Alcester, and on approaching Ragley Hall he dropped down low so that we could see the lovely view of the hall, and Lin again started screaming, but we soon landed and she climbed out, and told me that she would never do that again.

When we lived in Shaldon, I had a very good friend called Gordon Hook, who had 2 trawlers operating out of Brixham.

My son Paul asked me if I would talk to him and see if it was possible for him to go out fishing with him, and if he liked it he might have a job on the trawler.

I spoke with Gordon and he said it wasn't a problem, he could go anytime, so it was arranged and he went out with them on a 10 day trip to Liverpool Bay where Gordon often used to fish.

When he returned I asked him how he had got on, and he told me that it was so rough, he couldn't sleep, and had to work all hours, so I don't think that was the job for him.

Gordon had a set of salmon seine nets which had been handed down through his family, and that was licenced to him, and allowed him to row out into the estuary of the Teign, and then he had to make a circular movement without stopping in the water, until he reached the bank, and then haul the nets in, and see what they had caught. I have seen him catch 22 salmon at one time, when the tide was right and the salmon were running.

He then put the nets in the boat and left them for the next trip.

One day he told me that the nets had been pinched from the boat and, he knew who had done it, as he had some fishers in Teignmouth who were jealous of him.

He said he had told them to put them back in his boat otherwise there would be trouble, and he was a very hard man too!.

We were playing snooker in the conservative club one Saturday, and I told him I had to go to the toilet, and upon my return I was amazed to see one guy laid flat out on the floor and Gordon standing over him with a snooker cue.

The guy came to, and started to get up, and Gordon told him that if his nets were not back in his boat by tomorrow he would get more than that.

Suddenly the nets were found to be back in his boat, and all carried on as before!!

He told me the story about when he was out trawling one day, and suddenly he had no control of the boat, it was swinging backwards, forwards and sideways and he could do nothing about it.

Suddenly he looked out and a conning tower appear out of the water, and he realised that he had been caught by a submarine. Some sailors got out of the sub, cut the nets away from his trawler, and then disappeared.

He then claimed for 2 sets of nets from the Admiralty, and carried on fishing.

About 8 years later he was invited to some dinner which had been arranged in Plymouth, so he attended and suddenly, a guy came up to him and asked him if he had a trawler, Gordon replied that he did, and then the guy said I know the name of your trawler, because I was the captain of the submarine that caught you some years ago. They then became very good friends, and kept in touch with each other, and Gordon got an invite to go and look around the submarine.

He used to catch some salmon and sell them to the old ladies in the village at a good price, but when they took the fish, he told them that they didn't want to see the heads, and chopped them off and put them into a bag.

On Saturday mornings, we used to go round to his house and play cards, and he used to provide salmon sandwiches with loads of salmon, as there was so much meat in the cheeks of the fish, that we had plenty.

One weekend in Shaldon, we arranged a birthday party for Lin, and we went to the local hotel, "The Royal Standard", and my mother and father had come down from the midlands, and Lin's mother and father were there too.

We had been there a long time enjoying ourselves, and the drink was flowing well, and suddenly the door opened and in walked Tommy Cooper and his wife.

He was very tall, and his wife was very tall and a large lady. They went to the bar and ordered large gin and tonics, and we got chatting to them, and he told us that he was appearing at the Princess Theatre in Torquay the following week, and thought they would pop out for a quiet drink.

I told him that he had always been my idol and he then started to tell a few jokes. One of the locals then asked "Mr Cooper, can I tell you a joke?"

He then proceeded to tell this boring story, and Tommy told him to tell it again.."Just like that"!. He told it again and again, not realising that Tommy was taking the mickey!!. The whole pub was in uproar.

They must have had about 10 large gin and tonics, said their goodbyes, and left.

Lin and I had decided that we would go to London to see " The Buddy Holly Story", which was on at one of the theatres.

As we had been working with Landrover CKD, we became very friendly with several of the guys at Gaydon, and I told one of them that we were off to London that weekend, and he told me that I could use one of their Range Rovers, if I wanted. I thanked him and went and collected it from Gaydon, complete with a full tank of fuel

We drove to the hotel, parked the car and checked in. Later we got a taxi to the theatre, and watched a great show, as we both liked Buddy Holly, and it was a lovely evening.

The next day I told Lin that I would like to listen to some jazz, and so I phoned around to Ronnie Scott's and a few other places without success.

I then thought that the guy who would know where to go would be the doorman, so I went down and spoke with him, and he suggested that we go to the 100 club in Oxford Street. He got us a taxi and off we went, and when we got there we had to go downstairs to a small club, but there was lots of trad jazz music being played so it seemed to be the place.

Later in the evening there was a band called "The Mark Seymour Jump Band", and I thought that they were superb.

Our daughter Karen was getting married shortly, and I told Lin that I was going to speak with Mark Seymour at the interval, so I got up and went to see him.

I asked him if they did any outside gigs, and he said as long as they were not north of Birmingham, so I told him we were just south, so in principal he agreed to play for us on the agreed date.

I kept in touch with him and he gave us a listing of the music he would play, so all was great.

I then spoke with Joe and told him that I was thinking of going to France to buy all the duty free booze for the wedding so he decided to come with me.

I hired a van and we went on the ferry to Calais, where we found a large supermarket and spent a few hours choosing all the champagne, wines spirits and beers. We then drove back and unloaded all the contents into the snooker room in the bar.

Back at home we had decided to hold the reception in the paddock at the rear of our house, with a big marquee teeing off the snooker room up there, which had a bar inside.

I then organised a very swish mobile toilet with candelabras and music playing which was placed adjacent to the marquee.

The next thing was to organise the food, so I searched around and we found a small local company run by 2 sisters, and we had a meeting and discussed the menu, and finally decided on the total deal.

For the day I asked Ken, who worked in the local pub, if he would serve behind the bar for me, which he agreed. On the morning of the wedding I was getting dressed up, when Ken came running down and said he had a problem with the bar, so I ran up the top with him, and found that he had tapped a barrel of beer, and it had exploded all over the ceiling.

We spent the next hour cleaning it all up, to look spic and span for the event.

He worked very hard behind the bar as there were about 150 people there and it was all free drinks!!

After the wedding ceremony, everyone arrived at the marquee for the reception, and Mark Seymour had everything ready to commence the music, and I thought that I had chosen the music, and I just hoped that everyone would enjoy, but was a bit worried in case.

However when they started playing, everyone got to the floor and started dancing and I was very relieved.

We had organised a friend to come and record the music, and after it had finished he rushed off, and came back with recorded CD's for the family, and a tape for every other guest, which went down very well. We had previously prepared and printed the graphic covers for the CD's and tapes, together with a picture of the married couple on the covers.

The biggest problem I had was to get all the youngsters to leave as they were enjoying the bash, and together with the free booze, they had decided to stay as long as possible.

At about 2.00am, I went back up to the marquee, and gave then each a bottle of fizz and told them to shove off!!

The weather was kind to us, and it turned out to be a wonderful day.

Lin's mother and father decided to sell the hotel they had, so I suggested to them that they could come and live with us in the new annexe we had built, so her father soon packed his case and they moved and settled in with us, which was very good as they were a lovely couple.

They used to come with us quite often, and when we had the apartment in Palma, I asked them if they would like to come with us.

They both had never flown, and enjoyed the trip, and we spent 10 days there enjoying both the weather and the meals out.

We were out at Mario's one evening and enjoying a lovely meal along with a nice bottle of Rioja, and it came round to the desert menu. George, Lin's father looked at the menu and decided he would like the whisky ice cream cake, so I ordered our deserts, along with George's request from Fernando our friendly waiter.

The dishes arrived and placed in front of us and then Fernando arrived with a bottle of whisky, and started pouring it all over George's dish. It was slowly filling up and I told him that he had to tell the waiter when to stop.

By this time his dish was almost full, but he started plodding through it, and we finished the meal and set off back to the apartment.

When we got back George said he felt a bit tipsy, and then collapsed onto the settee. I finished up by undressing him and putting him to bed, and he wished me thank you and goodnight!

Later in the week, he was looking over the balcony, which looked out onto the bay, and also down to a communal swimming pool, which was two floors below .

Apparently in his earlier years he was a very good swimmer but being over 80, he had not swam for many a year, but he decided that he was going down and test the water.

I had to go to town to get a few supplies, and upon my return, I opened the door to the apartment and heard some shouting, so looked over the balcony to find that Lin was in the pool with her father, struggling to get him out. When she pulled him up out of the water, his head was up, but then he pulled her head back down in the water too. They were both in trouble.

I ran to the lift and grabbed a pool net that was handy and almost knocked one of the residents over in my panic, and shot down to the pool.

I held the pool net over for Lin to grab, and dragged her to the side, so she could hold on, then did the same for George, but that was a bit more of a problem, but eventually I did get him out of the pool.

Lin's mum was standing by the pool and shouted to him "Don't be silly and get out of that pool", which did nothing to help the situation.

We all got back into the apartment and calmed down, and thought how lucky we had been to rescue him and Lin from the pool.

As he went to bed, he went over and kissed Lin goodnight, and said" Thank you for saving my life…goodnight!!"

The rest of the week we did manage to be a bit more restrained and enjoyed the remaining part of our holiday.

Chapter 6

SHOOTING AND FISHING

Later that year it was Lin's mother May's birthday and as it was her 80th, we decided to arrange to do a surprise birthday party for her and get all the family together.

I spoke with all the members of the family, and fortunately, they were all able to make the party, so I arranged a Sunday at the Kings Court Hotel in Alcester, but she thought that it was just going to be a lunch with Lin, myself her and George.

I had asked all the family to be there early, so that they could be seated in the restaurant when we arrived. I grabbed her arm and said "come on mum, lets go and eat".

As we opened the door to the restaurant. She looked round and said "I think I know some of these people"!!.. to which I replied.. "I should think so..they are all your family"

It turned out to be a great party and she was inundated with flowers and chocolates, and she was so happy to see them all.

A bit later, I said "Come on mum, and have a look at the gardens", (as she loved gardening), and led her outside to walk around.

She enjoyed the gardens, and then asked me what the helicopter was doing in the grounds, so I suggested that we go and have a look and find out.

Unbeknown to her I had arranged for a friend of mine called Dennis Woodhams, who owned a helicopter to land there, and then take her up for a ride.

As we approached the helicopter, Dennis saluted her and she thanked him, and then he invited her to have a look inside He lifted her inside, and one of the young lads in the family climbed in too, and then they took off and we saw her waving from the window like the queen.

He flew her around for the next ½ hour and when they landed, she thanked him, and said how much she enjoyed the flight.

Then when she was 90, I arranged for her to go on a flight on Concorde, flying from Birmingham, and flying round the coast and back.

It then turned out that Lin and her sister Brenda wanted to go too, so I changed the numbers and Karen and I took them all to the airport and stood on the balcony there whilst they took off. I said to Karen "Silly me, that should have been all of us", but anyway they all enjoyed it and they were all given a commemorative pack to prove that they had been on Concorde.

It was not much longer after, that Concorde was stopped flying, so a great experience for them all.

Dennis Woodhams owned the local Arrow Mill hotel and restaurant, and we spent many happy times there, with parties and Sunday lunches.

One day he phoned me and said come for a drink tomorrow morning at about 12, so off I went and we got drinks from the bar and he said "Lets go outside, as it is a nice day"

When we got outside a helicopter flew into sight and then landed on the lawns, and the pilot got out and he introduced me to one of his best flying friends, as they were both in the Fleet Air Arm flying helicopters, and Dennis explained that he was now teaching others to fly. He had a pupil with him and he had just done 20 hours with him and was gaining experience.

Dennis then spoke with him on one side and told me that he was going to show me how he could operate the machine. He told me to get a pint sleever glass from the bar and hold it out horizontally. His friend then took off and came towards me and hovered, and then one of the skid type shoes entered the glass and he moved backwards and away about 30 yards, then moved back and put the glass back into my hand. Such a skill and incredible to experience.

Another time Dennis phoned me and told me to be there for exactly 11.50 am, and when I asked why, he told me that I would see.

We got a drink from the bar and then went outside and he said there and we looked up, and suddenly the Red Arrows appeared, and flew low over the hotel and circled a few times, whilst waving from the cockpit.

He then told me that he knew the team leader well, as he had flown with him and they were good friends, and as they were going off to an event in Wales he asked them to fly over for us.

I was later invited to the hotel, as he had both the Red Arrows team leader and his number 2, staying at the hotel for a meal, so I joined them and listened to all their interesting stories which were very enlightening.

I joined the Coughton shoot, along with my friend Joe, and met all the other guns, and this shoot carried on for some 12 years, before people moved on and it no longer operated as a shoot.

We had 4 x 2 paired syndicate members, the idea being that when it became a pair's day for the shoot, it was up them to take it in turns to look after the day, which meant providing the drinks for the day, and then arranging the lunch for the 8 members and 2 guests, and all the beaters, which was normally back at the barn.

Then in the evening, had to provide the meal for the 10 guns at their own house, so a lot of work for the wives.

We used to assemble at Bob Colletts farm buildings where we had a bacon sandwich, with coffees and brandies, and then on to the four drives of the morning, being Sadlers, The Dry Pit, The Game Cover and then the Oak wood, then returning to the barn for sandwiches and drinks.

After lunch we set off again and did the three drives of the afternoon, being Top of the Park, The Park over the Road, and lastly The Wet wood.

We normally had a few drinks between the drives, such as champagne or Sloe gin to keep the cold out!!

Then back to the barn to sort the birds out and total the bag for the day, which was anything from 60 to 250 birds, which included pheasants and partridge.

The keeper Ken did a great job in looking after all the young chicks when they arrived, and then ensuring that all vermin was kept under control

He used to arrange for the team of beaters, and make sure they arrived on time for the commencement of the shoot.

We used to put down a total of approximately 2500 birds per season and shoot approximately 50 percent.

We had some great days shooting and not without incident most days.

I remember one shoot drawing to a close, and all the guns lining up to shoot the Wet Wood. One of the guests was placed on no 10 peg, which was on the extreme right of the drive, and he was told not to shoot anything that went past him on the right. The reason being that there was the old station house which had been converted into a house and was being lived in, so it would have been dangerous to shoot in that direction.

However the birds started flying well, and he just could not resist it and his gun went up and over his right shoulder, and shot a pheasant, which then crashed through the kitchen window and was running round the kitchen of this house.

Joe the shoot team leader laced into him for doing it after he had been told about it, and banned him from the shoot in future.

Joe and I then had to go over to the house and apologise profusely for the damage caused, and despatch the bird, which had spread blood all over their kitchen. Fortunately the guy was very understanding and provided we paid for the damage, he told us he would not take it any further.

Joe had to claim on our insurance policy, which increased the premium for the following season, adding more to the total each gun had to pay.

Another time I was responsible for organising the day, so the evening meal was to be held at our cottage, arranged for a start of 6.30pm.

All the guns arrived and as usual they all started drinking and chatting about the day, and before the meal they had consumed 4 bottles of gin and one bottle of whisky, together with some wine!

Lin and daughter Karen then produced a wonderful meal with roast beef and all the trimmings, and the guns then consumed 13 bottles of wine, and finished up with some port, until I ran out.

The evening finished and the guns started to depart, most of them having arranged lifts to get them home, but one gun, Henry said he was driving home in his Landrover.

Well he got into his Landrover and drove out of the drive and landed in the ditch directly opposite, and then tried again and did exactly the same thing, before we convinced him that we would get him a lift home, so we got his Landrover back into the drive and fixed him up with a lift.

They were some very good days and we all became very good friends.

Joe had been telling me about his salmon fishing trips in Scotland, and I got very interested but had never fly fished before, and also I need an invite to go, as the fishing rights on the River Helmsdale, in the Highlands, was owned by 6 Landowners.

The fishing consisted of 25 miles of river and was split into 6 beats below, and 6 beats above, and the middle of the beats had a fishing lodge to determine the centre.

One owner was a very good friend of ours called Patrick, and he owned a section of the river and so this was how Joe got his invite to fish there. He had been going up there for a period of 2 years, and spoke to Patrick and told him that I was interested in going if there was any chance.

So one evening in the local pub, Patrick told me that there was a space and I was invited if I would like to go.

I jumped at the chance, as the river was known to be one of the best salmon rivers in the country.

I arranged the trip, as I would be there for a week, leaving home early on Sunday morning and returning the following Sunday.

I thought that I had best get some fly fishing lessons. And so as there was the Royal Show on, I went there, as I was told there was a lake with a fisherman, giving private lessons. So off I go and introduced myself to this man, and spent 3 hours with him, mastering the art. I felt very proud to think that I had got the hang of fly fishing.

The week was arranged for the trip and having bought all the necessary rods and kit, Joe told me that he would drive over in his RangeRover and pick me up at 5.00am the following Sunday.

He duly arrived and we loaded all my gear, together with wines, spirits and beers we needed for the week. Then Joe went and sat in the passenger seat, and told me that I was a better driver then him so I could drive.

We set off for the 8 hour trip, and Joe was fast asleep by the time we had hit the main road. I had the radio on for company, and from time to time Joe did open his eyes, but soon closed them again.

The traffic was not bad and I wanted to get to Tebay services in Cumbria as the next stop, to get a bacon roll and some coffee, and have a break for a few minutes.

Our 2 friends from Oxford, who were fishing with us, phoned me and we arranged to meet at Tebay, as they were not far behind us on the M6.

After our break, we all set off again and this time the plan was to go to a restaurant called The Oystercatcher at a place called Portmahamack, on the east coast, where we had arranged lunch. We arrived there at 1.10pm, after driving 512 miles with the one break.

The restaurant was very good, run by Sue, the waitress owner, and her husband the French chef.

The menu arrived and had some lovely choices, including lobster as the main course. Joe ordered lobster and was told that sorry but they had run out, but if he could wait 20 minutes there would be a fresh supply, as the harbour was directly opposite, and they delivered daily. It duly arrived and so we all ate together.

Joe asked me to order the wine so I asked for the winelist, and was given a book with about 40 pages of listings of wines. I looked through and said I had found a nice wine, and he told me to order it.

I said I think you had better look at the winelist first, and when he saw the price, which was £1245, he quickly told me to order the house wine and close the book!! Apparently the French chef bought and collected wines, and had a large stock, and every year he agreed with his accountant to write some of the stock off, as this was a nice tax dodge!

We had a superb lunch and then set off to Helmsdale, which was about 40 miles away, and got there without problems, pulling up at the Tigh an Ab fishing lodge.

We had separate rooms, so we unloaded our cases, and then settled down in the lounge to relax.

We waited for the live in chef, Derek, to arrive as he was due at about 5.30pm, and he duly arrived and settled in to his room, setting up all the kitchen and getting the food stocks in to the fridges and freezers.

He then said that we would be having a salad that evening with deserts, and cheese and biscuits. We sat down at about 7.00pm, and enjoyed a lovely meal with some wine to wash it down with.

We then went to our rooms, as we were all tired from the long trip, and wanted to be bright and ready the next morning for the start of the days fishing.

We agreed to meet at 6.00am in the morning, and Derek cooked us a lovely breakfast, and then loaded all the gear we needed for the day and set off to meet our Ghillies down on the river. The beat we were on that day was not far from the lodge, so we soon arrived there and I was introduced to Johnnie, and Gill, as the other guys had been fishing with them before.

We split into 2 parties, as the rules state that Joe and I would fish the beat below, and the other guys would fish the beat above, which meant that the lodge was in the middle, with the beats either side, 12 miles each way.

Joe started fishing first as it was only allowed to fish one rod at a time, so he went with Johnnie and I watched from the bank. He soon hooked a fish and after some time he landed it, and it turned out to be a small 6lb salmon.

He carried on and then told me to come down, as it was my turn to fish. I got my rod and Johnnie took it and put a fly on, and said to me "show me what you can do". I told him I had taken some lessons, so off I went and cast the line across the river. He told me to cast again and then stopped me and said " I think we best start again", in his lovely Scottish accent.

He then taught me how to fish, and at the end of the week, he told me that I had done very well, which was due to his vast experience. The best part was when I caught my first fish, which was a 12 lb salmon, which took about 35 minutes to land, finishing up with Johnnie kneeling down at the water's edge, and easing the landing net around the fish. He then held the fish and with some blood on his fingers, he rubbed it across my forehead, which was always the thing to do, after catching the first fish. This was called blooding! I was now a proper fisher!!

One day I was fishing and I was in the river in my waders, and casting out up the river with johnnie by my side, and we saw so many fish running that he told me we must catch some.

I was concentrating very hard and had several bites, but they would not take the fly.

Suddenly a voice behind me said "Hello there how is the fishing going?". I took no notice as I was watching my line with the fish running. Then the voice said it again. We had come to the end of the beat by then, so I turned round waded towards the bank, and looked up at the man standing there.

I could not believe it, as standing there was Prince Charles, and when I reached the bank, he wanted to know how the fishing was, as he was fishing the river the following day. We chatted for about 15 minutes, and then he walked off to his RangeRover, driven by his security guy.

I later found out from Johnnie, that he always used to fish the Helmsdale every year, as Lady Diana's sister, Sarah

McCorquodale owned a part of the river, but after Diana died, he was banned, and this was his first return to the river.

We had good weather all week, and the fishing was superb, finishing up with 32 salmon between us, as then you were able to take the total catch home, but now you are only allowed 1 fish each, as there is a catch and release rule in operation.

Whilst we were there, Johnnie took us to the Hatchery, which was very interesting. At the end of the season, all the Ghillies get together and catch all the hen fish they can, using prawns, then milk the fish to get all the eggs , and then they put them into a series of tanks, with the small eggs in the first, and then as they grow, they move them to the next tank. When they are ready they take them and put them back into the burns that they came from to be ready for the next season

I continued to go to Helmsdale for the next 15 years with Joe, fishing for the week, and we had some wonderful eventful times, and I am still in touch with Johnnie the Ghillie now.

Chapter 7

PRANK ON VINCE

We used to frequent the Rossini restaurant in Alcester which was owned by Vincenzo D'Elia, who became a very good friend as well as a very good restauranteur. When I first started the business, the premises were on the Eclipse Trading Estate, and close by there was a post office and café. Vince bought this and the converted it to the Rossini restaurant.

We had some great times there with friends for years, and even then the price was about £40 per head, whatever you had to eat!

He was very fond of the ladies and when Lin and I went there, he would kiss Lin and fondle her bottom, which got him a smack, but he did this with all the ladies.

He really knew his wines, and had a wonderful wine cellar at his house, and used to sell wines to the public too.

He then bought some premises in Alcester in the high street, which he converted to a café, and upstairs a small restaurant. The building was very old, and the stairs were very tricky to climb, and once upstairs, the floor was very uneven, and you had to be careful how you walked.

A crowd of us had a meal there one night, and I was sitting on a chair on a very bad part of the floor, and halfway through the evening, the chair tipped me over and I fell to the floor, and bruised my back.

Vince came over and asked me if I was ok, and I told him it was a bit painful. We paid up and left, and the next day

I thought I would play a prank with him, as he was always doing it to us.

I wrote a fake solicitors letter and sent it to him (copy attached), and when he received the letter he phoned me and was very upset. He apologised and asked me to phone my solicitor and cancel it. I said I would not.

He then must have phoned his solicitor, who told him it was a joke, as he then phoned me and called me all the names he could think of!!

The next time we went for a meal, he tried to charge me extra for the wine, but that was a joke which he didn't get away with!

Lin and I went there one Sunday with my brother and his wife, and we were sitting and chatting after the meal, and my brother told me that Steve Bruce, the then Birmingham City manager had just arrived. When Vince came over, I said that he had a celebrity in tonight, and he asked who, so I told him. He said he had never heard of him.

Within a few minutes he went over to him and shouted loudly, "Hey Stevie, so good to see you here", and that was Vince!

Conyer, Large & Mount

Pound House Mob: 07813 924014
Checkitt Lane
Bromsgrove
Worcs
WR2 8UO

Solicitors
Personal Claims Specialists

Attn Mr Vincenzo D'Elia
Rossini Lavinotec
11 Church Street
Alcester
Warks
B49 5AH

5th February 2010

Dear Sir

I am writing on behalf of our client Mr R.Hughes, who dined with some friends at your restaurant on Saturday 30th January 2010, and was involved in an incident by falling from his chair, causing severe bruising and damage to his Gluteus Maximus.

I am informed that this was caused by an uneven floor and a slippery chair covering, and although Mr Hughes had consumed alcohol prior to this event, the main cause would appear to be due to the uneven floor, as with an older type property such as yours, this is often the case.

Under the Health and Safety Act 1974, it requires risk assessments for all the appropriate concerns, and there should be adequate notices placed, to show any potential problems. As I am informed there are no notices of this type on display.

Mr Hughes has been unable to attend his offices, and more importantly, has not been able to walk or sit for the past few days, and this would appear to be an ongoing situation.

I would hope that we could discuss some form of settlement, as I am sure you would not want any unnecessary disruption to your business by investigation, which could lead to litigation.

Please feel free to contact me on the above mobile number, as I am out of office most days.

Yours Sincerely

I Conyer   LLB

Conyer, Large & Mount, Solicitors

Registered in England No—1234123

Chapter 8

BRAKE PADS

During the late 70's and 80's the Automotive industry was producing so many cars, and as they were not selling as fast, they decided to store them on disused airfields, and anywhere they could find space.

I was contacted by the purchase manager, who was a friend of mine at Lucas Girling, and he asked if I would be interested to attend a meeting at their offices in West Bromwich.

They explained that they had been asked by the manufacturers to solve a problem that had occurred during the storage of the cars.

The problem was that as they were standing for a long period, sometimes with grass growing under the vehicles, the brake discs had become very rusty.

Then when they delivered the cars to the dealers, the brakes squealed and the customers were not impressed, assuming there was a fault with the car.

They asked all the brake manufacturers to see what they could do to resolve the problem

Ferodo Brakes had already produced a remedy, so Girling had arranged a visit to their factory to see how this had been done. I was asked that if they could get the details for this, would I be interested in doing the work for them. I agreed if it was possible to be done.

I went with the Girling team and I wore a white coat with the Girling logo on, so it was assumed that I worked for Girling.

At the visit, we were shown some brake pads which had been treated, and they had two small strips of a cure affixed to the brake pad, which when fitted to the vehicle, and the brakes applied, the strips rubbed against the discs, and removed all the rust that had occurred, thereby resolving the squeal, After a few miles the two strips had worn off, as it was only 3mm thick, and the pad was back to its original shape.

We were then showed the mix for the two strips, and how it was applied to the brake pads.

I obtained all the ingredients for this treatment, and also how they applied it, and then into an industrial oven, baking the cure to the pads.

I then went back, and thought how this could be done in our factory, and the biggest problem was how to apply the mix to the pads,

I contacted a toolmaker I knew and asked him if he could produce a tool for me and within a week, he came back with a small machine and showed me how it could be done.

Four disc pads were placed in the bed of the machine, then a cover was brought down onto the pads. This cover held a sheet of plastic, which had strips cut out of the plastic, so that a mix could be screened across the pads, applying through the cutouts.

The cover was then taken off, and the pads removed and placed onto a backing plate, to move to the oven for heat treatment, which was for about 3 hours.

After we did some trials, we settled on the process we needed, and I went back to Girling with a price to receive the pads, apply the abrasive strips, heat treat them, and then pack the pads into the Girling cartons, and return them to

Girling. They accepted the price and gave me an open order to commence as soon as I could get everything in place.

I had to purchase two ovens, as they could only hold 240 pads, so they were soon delivered and I had been able to purchase all the ingredients required, so we were in a position to commence.

The ingredients include a resin, talcum powder, and a couple of other items, which was quite a simple mix.

We produced the first batch of 50 pads, which I took to Girling and they fitted them to some vehicles, and tested them, and said that they were happy with the results.

We then started to produce batches of pads and pack them and ship to Girling and eventually we were producing 15,000 pads month, which at the price quoted made us a very healthy profit, and helped us to then move on to another larger unit on the estate.

We then had other contracts, and things went well.

Chapter 9

SPOOF

Every Friday I had to drive down to Unipart in Oxford, for a morning meeting to discuss the current situation, and for any new work they wanted to add to the packing contract.

After the meeting I took the Purchase Director John out to lunch, and he loved to go to the George Hotel in Dorchester, as one of his friends owned the hotel.

We used to have a very long lunch, and one day Gerry the owner suggested that we play a game of spoof for a car which he had outside in his garage.

He had another friend in the hotel, so the four of us sat down and he told us the rules. The game was to cost us £400 each, and the winner would be able to take the car, but he would not tell us what car it was.

Anyway we all had a nice boozy lunch, so we all began to play the game, and one by one guys dropped out, and I was left with Gerry to decide the winner.

The game went on with neither of us guessing the correct number, so off we went again, until I called spoof and won the game.

He then took me outside and opened up his garage, to find a 1941 Willys Jeep, in perfect condition with the star on the bonnet and a jerry can and shovel strapped to the side. I couldn't believe my luck, and told Jerry that I would come back at the weekend to collect it, which he agreed was fine.

By then it was time to get the John back to his office to collect his briefcase and he then told me to follow him to Austin Rover No 2 production factory, just round the corner.

We arrived and went inside and he then took me upstairs where there was a bar and 3 snooker tables. There were men playing snooker and John told me that they were the production managers from the factory.

We were enjoying a drink when the phone rang and a voice behind the bar asked for one of the managers. He went to the phone and after a few minutes we heard him say "So you have a problem on the line…you sort it…that's what you are paid for", and put the phone down.

John said that it happened many times, which just showed what the management was like in those times, especially with Red Robbo controlling things from Longbridge.

We left after about an hour and I set off back home, glad that I was not involved with the Rover guys at that time, but not aware that I would be dealing with them at a much later date.

At the weekend I was driven down to Dorchester with my son Paul to collect the Jeep, and we drove it back home with many greetings from passing cars.

I used to take it to the local boy's club, and show them, and drive them around in it, which they loved.

About a year later I sold it for £1000, which I put into the business, so a very successful game of spoof.

Chapter 10

HOLIDAYS

We have had some wonderful holidays either on our own or with Joe and Barbara.

We booked one to Penang, which entailed flying to Singapore, then transferring to Penang, Malaysia. We stayed in a hotel called The Rasa Sayang, which is in the Shangri-La group of hotels. I think that it is one of the best hotels that I have stayed in.

We liked to eat out in the evenings as opposed to eating in the hotel, and we found a restaurant nearby called The Ferringhi Garden, so we booked a table and went along.

It was a lovely restaurant, and we decided to use it for evening meals, and we soon got to know the owners, Richard and Evelyn Long, who were Chinese Malays. They made us very welcome and could not do enough for us.

As we used the place every evening, Richard said that he would send a minibus to collect us, which he arranged, and when it arrived it was driven by a 6ft 5 Japanese man who was called Mr Woo. We soon go to know him too.

I asked Richard, why a Japanese man was working for him, and he told me that he used to own a labour supply company, and he found Mr Woo. Apparently he had a very prosperous business in Tokyo, and the problem was that his wife was spending more than he could earn. So he just upped and left everything, left Japan and turned to drink, and then Richard found him, and straightened him out, finally working for him at the restaurant. He was a lovely man and would do anything for you.

Richard asked us one evening what we would be doing the next day, and we told him that we had decided to drive over the bridge, and drive to the Thailand border and see what we could do from there. When we go to the border they would not let us over as we did not have the papers for the car, so we spent some time in duty free, and left to drive back.

On the way we found a nice little restaurant, where we had a lovely lunch, along with some beers and wine. Off we went again, and stopped a few times on the way for some beers, arriving back at the hotel. That evening we went to the Ferringhi, and Richard asked us where we had been, we explained what we had done, and he said you mean that you have been drinking. I said yes just a few, to which he replied that in Penang if you are found to be driving with more than a half of beer, they strip you to your underpants, and throw you down in the cells with all the pimps and prostitutes. We decided not to do that again!!

One day the girls said they would like to do some shopping, so Richard said he would take us to a shopping centre in Georgetown, the capital of Penang.

We got there and we entered the centre, and then climbed on a moving staircase to the upper floors. Lin had on a loose flimsy skirt on and as the staircase moved upwards she realised that her skirt was trapped in the moving gear. She tried to remove it, but could not, and so when we got to the top all she had on was a top and a scanty pair of panties!

We made a quick dart to the nearest shop to buy her another skirt, after all the people smiling at her predicament.

Richard then took us to his favourite Chinese restaurant, where we had a magnificent meal, finished off with a huge dish placed on the table in front of us, which when the cover was removed I could see what looked like some coiled springs from a settee!. It turned out to be a delicacy, which was sharks intestines, but as long as you closed your eyes when eating it, it was very tasty.

On another one of our planned trips we decided to drive to a ferry about 60 miles away, and then cross to an island called Pangkor Laut, where we had booked in for a couple of days. We arrived there and they showed us to our rooms, which was in cabins, suspended over the sea on stilts. We sat outside on the decking, enjoying a nice drink, and enjoying the sun and the sound of the sea.

The bathroom had a glass floor and so did the bath, so when you bathed you could see the water underneath you, which was quite different.

We drove around the island, which was not very big and not a great deal to see, but it was still an enjoyable stay.

On another one of our trips we flew to Thailand and stayed in Phuket for a couple of days, and then flew to an island called Ko Samui, where we stayed for a further 2 days. When we landed they collected with a small tractor which towed some small trailers which carried us and the luggage. The hotel was quite basic, but the staff and facilities were excellent.

We tried a few places to eat and the food was very good, mainly seafood.

Joe saw an advert for a snake show, and although the girls were not too keen, we went. When we got there we had to sit on seats overlooking a pit which was about 20 feet below. The show started and a man came in with 2 cobras, and put them down on the floor and then they proceeded to attack his legs, biting him. He just stood there and we were then told that as he had done this so many times, his body had become immune to the poison. Quite a different show!

During the interval we bought some beers and enjoyed the sunshine, and then the second half started. A man came in and had a wicker type hamper, and then he opened the top, grabbed a snake, and threw it in my direction. I was up and running so fast, and then he explained that it was a rubber snake, and everyone burst out with laughter, whilst my heart was racing"!!

We then flew back to Phuket, where we got the flight back home, after a very enjoyable break.

HOLIDAYS—2

Lin and I loved to go to Antigua, staying in a resort called Galley Bay.

We drove to Gatwick, checked in the Hilton hotel, then walked out of the hotel and along to the airport, where we checked in the evening before, and returned to the hotel, and enjoyed a lovely meal, before retiring to bed. The next morning we just walked along to the airport, and went through security and on to the plane for the flight.

The flight was quite long, but Virgin made us very welcome, and the hours quickly passed.

Landing at St John's airport we got a taxi and a quick ride to the resort, where we checked in and shown to our rooms, which were right on the beach.

We soon found our way around, and enjoyed all the facilities there, and meeting some lovely people, some of which we are still in touch with.

We used to have breakfast and then at around 11 o'clock, we would get in the pool, and call the waiter, who would then provide us with glasses of champagne, and in those days they were proper glasses The friends we had made then saw what was going on and before long I had called it the 11 o'clock club and it finished up with about 12 people in the pool.

One day we were enjoying as usual, and suddenly a voice said "Excuse me but what is going on there", to which I replied it was the 11 o'clock club.

I then saw that he was an Englishman and had a suit, tie and shoes on, but he then said " Do you mind if I join you?". At that point he jumped in fully dressed, and I handed him a glass of champers. Then within minutes his wife appeared fully dressed and did the same. Eccentric English!!!

I was chatting with an Australian that we became friendly with, and he said that he enjoyed fly fishing, and I told him that I did enjoy it too, and he said he had booked a fly fishing trip to Barbuda, the sister island. I said I would be interested too, so he gave me the details, and I booked to go along with him.

It meant that we were to fly in a small plane over to Barbuda, and then on to fly fish on a coral bed with about 9 inches of water covering the coral. We had T shirts and shorts, and we had to wear sandals or some foot coverings, as the coral was very sharp to the feet.

We landed and the airport terminal was a 40ft container, and one man checking to make sure we were not a problem!

We had a guy with us who told us where to go to start fishing, and so we started to get the fly working over the water. After just a few casts, we saw what we came to fish for and that was bonefish. They were incredible to see, as they came out of the water to take the fly and then they became transparent,.

It was a great 4 hours fishing and we caught a lot of fish, taking some back to the resort, where they cooked them for us, but not much taste.

We met another English couple, and enjoyed their company, when Jane told me that I looked like her father, and would I do her the honour of giving her away as they were getting married in 2 days time. I felt very honoured, and agreed.

On the day, I had to go along to her room at the other end of the beach, collect her, and then walk her along the boardwalk to the small chapel close to reception.

The wedding went off very well and we all enjoyed the reception afterwards, and we still keep in touch with them nowadays.

I was talking with the manager, and he told me that they arrange helicopter trips to Montserrat, to see the volcano, and the damage it caused when it blew some years before.

I asked Lin and she said she would like to go, so I spoke with the manager, who organised the trip for the following day.

So we were taken to St John's airport to join the helicopter, and we flew to the island and around the perimeter of the volcano, which was still issuing some smoke, but obviously was not active. The pilot explained that when the volcano blew, the lava flowed down the island and covered the airport and the town, and you could see the path that it had taken. He then flew back low over the sea, and there was a school of dolphins leaping from the water, which was a beautiful sight.

We went to Antigua several more times and then decided to go to another resort, this time in Mexico.

I found a resort called El Dorado Royale, which was just outside Cancun.

We booked to go, and flew from Heathrow to Cancun, where we got a taxi to take us to the resort, which was about 40 minutes by road.

We arrived, and was taken to our room on the beach by golf buggy, where a butler showed us around and made sure we were comfortable. He also showed me the four optics in the room, and asked us which spirits we would like, so

I ordered some whisky and Gin, and he told me that they would check every day to top it up if necessary.

We also had 2 girls who acted as room service, so just a call to them and they would arrive and sometimes with the butler.

The service was fantastic and we soon found our way about, as there were some 13 restaurants, and 17 bars, but you need to call the transport to book a golf buggy to get you around as the distance between some of the facilities, was quite far.

We soon found our favourite places to go and got to know some of the waiters very well by name, and they looked after Lin especially very well, as she was not able to walk very far then.

Part of the package was a candle light dinner for 2 on the beach in the evening, and that was a bit special, as they provided superb service, and decorated the dishes with our names around the sides of the plates, and it usually was our wedding anniversary whilst there, so they really did us proud.

Another part of the package was to include a special meal at one of the restaurants, which had several Large TV screens around, and the idea was that they had a chef cook a meal, whilst explaining all the details, and you could also watch the screens to see how they did it.

They then cooked each course and then served the dish to you and at the same time they served wines to suit, and informed us all about the wines and where they were from.

We used to have a meal at one of the restaurants, then get a buggy back to the club house, where they held a show every evening, and had a large circular bar, with waiters serving us whatever drinks we required.

The butler had organised a beach hut for the daytime, if we wanted and so we used to go there and he would arrive with a coldbox filled with drinks and a buzzer, so that if we required anything more, all we had to do was to press the buzzer, and he appeared.

One day we were eating at one of our favourite restaurants, Jo Jo's, and I looked over to the far side of the restaurant and could not believe what I could see.

On one of the tables was my old friend Vince from Rossini's, with his wife Margaret, and their son.

I did not say a word to Lin and crept over to him, who was sitting with his back to us, and put my hands around his neck and said" I kill you, I kill you" in my best Italian accent, and he shrieked out and then I let go and he saw me and called me all the names under the sun. It was just one of those times that you enjoy getting your own back on someone!!

We went back to the resort several times, but as Lin was getting a big problem with her walking etc, we decided that longhaul flights was not for us anymore.

Chapter 11

LUFAPAK

When I sold the company to the group, all the Unipart and other motor business was transferred to Rugby where they operated from.

After about 2 years I was contacted by my Unipart director friend, who told me that they were looking to set up a packing operation in Germany, as they now had a warehouse there for their European distribution of parts.

He told me that they had been in touch with a company there, who was a small contract packer, and would we be interested in talking with them to form a joint business.

I put it to the board of the group, who seemed very interested, so after various phone calls, a meeting was set up at the German factory, and the director of the group and myself went there.

After lengthy meetings and visits, it was agreed that the group would buy shares in the company, and Lufapak then awarded the Unipart packing contract in Germany.

The factory was in a small town called Neuwied, which was not far from Koblenz.

At the start of the business, it was agreed that they needed the same type of computer system that we had in England, so I had to go over there with my IT manager twice a week to settle in and train the staff in the system.

At the first meeting I had there the managing Director, Harald Fuchsell, called all his staff to the conference room, and explained what would happen, and they all started speaking in German. Harald slammed his fist down on the table and said "No, we all speak in English from now on, with our colleagues from England".

I was very glad as I do not speak any German at all.

I soon got to know most of the staff, who turned out to be friends as well.

Harald invited me to his home and introduced me to his wife, and we enjoyed a lovely evening there.

Since then I have visited Germany with Lin for long weekends, where we met some of the staff, and had meals out with them.

I used to fly to Frankfurt, and then hire a car and drive about an hour to Koblenz, where we stayed in a hotel there.

One time we were there, and Harald was telling me about an event that takes place every year called "Rhein in Flammen".

Lin and I decided to book for this and so arrived at Koblenz, where we boarded a boat, and then have a very long lunch and watch a show on board the boat. Then late in the afternoon the boat takes off up the river to a place called Boppard, where it moors up for an hour, and you can get off and have a walk around the town if you want.

By then it is getting dark, and back on board the boat lights up being covered in bright coloured lights, and then slowly starts the return journey to Koblenz.

By this time there are many boats assembling around, all with brightly coloured lights, finishing up with about 80-100 boats all sailing closely together, and as they have a lot of red colours, it reflects in the river which looks red, hence the river on fire!!

Then as all the boats slowly sail, there are lots of places on the banks that have huge firework displays, which also light up the sky, so the sights are very impressive. There are a few castles high on the river banks, and they also have firework displays, so the whole of the river and sky is lit up.

The boat then arrives back at Koblenz, where it stops on the river, opposite castle called Ehrenbreitstein, where there is a grand finale of a firework display which lights up the sky and amazes everyone on board the boats, who come to visit from all over the world.

On our works visits with my IT manager, Chetan, we sometimes was there on a Friday, and so we would stop over for Saturday too, so that we could go and visit the local area, which was very enjoyable along both the Rhine and the Moselle rivers , which meet in Koblenz.

I really enjoyed our trips to Germany and are still in touch with Harald now, as a very good friend.

Chapter 12

LIN'S HEALTH

Lin has had back problems for a long time due to Osteoporosis, and Scoliosis, and eventually she had to have operations on her back to have metal rods inserted to keep her spine in place.

The first one was a small operation which had a rod inserted from the base of the spine and took about 2 hours in the Orthopaedic Hospital in Birmingham.

This helped, but as her spine was so fragile, she was always worried about falling and breaking something.

In 2006 I took her back to see Mr Alistair Thompson and Mr David Marks, who were the surgeons who operated on her, and they decided to perform another operation to extend the rods up to the top of her spine.

This was a very delicate operation and took 8.5 hours with both surgeons.

This helped a lot but after some time she complained of pain, so I took her to see them both again and they decided to have her scanned and they found that one of the screws fitting to the rods appeared to be loose, so again she went to hospital to have this screw removed.

All this surgery did help and without it she would not have been able to walk, albeit she now has to have a walking frame.

Since then she has had 2 strokes, which really knocked her about, and also she has had fractures, one of which was a really bad fracture of the pubic ramus, so that put her in hospital again.

The surgeon told me that her sacral fracture was like a polo mint which had shattered into many pieces, and had to have cement augmentation to secure the pieces back together again.

We used to see a consultant surgeon at the Q.E in Birmingham on a regular basis, but after a few years he told Lin that there was nothing more he could do for her and discharged her.

We then found out that she had contracted C.I.D.P. which is short for Chronic Demyelinating Polyneuropathy.

This meant that Lin finished up with tremendous hand tremors, leaving her unable to do anything with her hands, even to clean her own teeth.

We now have to employ carers for mornings and evenings to assist her with her personal hygiene.

So due to all these problems we are unable to go on holidays like we used to and just get small breaks when we can, with the wheelchair at the ready.

Chapter 13

COTTAGE FLOODING

When we lived in the cottage, there is a stream running at the rear of the property which takes all the water past, and on to a brook called Bow Brook. This then flows many miles across farmland.

In 2007 there was a period when we had tremendous storms, and so much rainfall that the stream could not cope with the amount of water, resulting in the cottage getting flooded with about 8 inches of water throughout the whole of the ground floor.

We had to get pumps in and heaters to dry out the cottage and we lived virtually upstairs for a period of about a month.

The insurance company were very good and helped us with lots of problems which we had to sort.

It was very nice to get back to normality at the end of that period.

Since we sold the cottage and built the existing house in the grounds, I had all the water course altered, with the permission of the Water Board, the Environmental Agency, and the local planning, so hopefully we will never have that problem again in the future.

Chapter 14

WORKSHOP FIRE

I started woodturning when I was in my forties and found it very enjoyable, so I had my own workshop built at the top of the garden, and gradually purchased various pieces of machinery that I need to produce many types of woodturning, such as Clocks, Barometers, Pens, Bowls, and many other pieces.

I finished up with a workshop full of machinery and stocks of all items that I need for the production of the finished products.

I had many years where I would just disappear into my workshop and spend many hours woodturning, which I found so relaxing, and very proud when I looked at the finished items, some of which I gave a birthday presents, Xmas presents, and many others I sold.

This went on for many years, until in December 2023, I was helping Lin to eat her breakfast, and looking out of the window, I saw some smoke billowing from the roof of the workshop.

I left Lin and hurried up the path, and just as I was about 15 yards away the whole of the workshop blew and there was a huge bang, and flames leaping into the air and hitting the trees in the wood right behind the workshop.

I had my phone with me and so I dialled 999 and within about 20 minutes, there were 3 fire engines arrived from local stations.

They could not get up to the workshop with their engines so they had to run the hoses all the way up which was about 125 yards.

I did manage to get my big ride on mower out of the next shed alongside the workshop, and one of the firemen told me I must not get as near as the smoke was getting very bad then.

They managed to douse the fire after a considerable time, but it was such a bad fire that when they had finished there was just a big molten mass of metal left on the floor.

I was amazed at the speed of the fire and just what it had burnt, as all of my machinery and all my stocks of parts and timber had gone.

The firemen thought that it must have been either a squirrel chewing through the cables of an electrical fault, which they detailed in their report.

I claimed on my insurance company, and they did very quickly agree and pay out the amount claimed.

Every time I went up to the mess, I had tears in my eyes, losing all my treasured machinery and stocks.

I did replace the workshop, but I have not replaced any machinery and have now decided not to do any more woodturning, which I thoroughly enjoyed.

www.ingramcontent.com/pod-product-compliance
Lightning Source LLC
Chambersburg PA
CBHW050306120526

44590CB00016B/2516